WOMENEMIES

And How to Eliminate Them

By Marilena Fallaris

Womenemies: *And How to Eliminate Them*

Copyright @ 2020 by Marilena Fallaris

Published in the United States by BCG Publishing, 2020.

http://www.BCGPublishing.com

Dedications

This book is dedicated to my mom, Katherine A. Dick, who has sacrificed so much to provide me with all the tools and support to pursue my dreams. She uplifts me and others around her. Whenever I hit rock bottom she's always there to pick me up and give me the motivation to keep pushing on. She always wants me to know that the world is my oyster. Thanks, Mom.

I also dedicate this book to my husband, Vasileios Psyrras, who verbally and emotionally supports me every day and gave me the confidence to share this book with the world. Vasileios is the epitome of loving what he does and helping others. Baby, you are a constant inspiration to me.

I dedicate this book to my father, who is now in heaven. My father always wanted me to be fearless and say what is on my mind. Well, this one is for you, Baba (Greek for dad).

I dedicate this book to my son Emmanuel. You give us a daily reason to be happy and filled with joy.

Finally, I dedicate this to all the positive women in my life—family members, colleagues, friends, and classmates—who exemplify the lessons in the book and help other women. You were my inspiration for writing this book.

Disclaimer

To the reader: Please note that these stories from my personal life are told from my perspective and how I interpreted the situation to have happened. Everyone has a different viewpoint of the same situation, which is part of what makes life so interesting. The point of the book is to explain how certain situations made me or my loved ones feel, and hopefully others can see how their actions, even if unintended, can have an impact on others—some negative and some positive.

Also, names and some facts have been changed as the identities are not important. What is important is discussing the existence of womenemies so we can figure out a solution to eliminate the problem of women treating each other negatively.

Table of Contents

Chapter 1

Why Write About Womenemies

Women have the capacity to bring so much joy to others and to the world. We carry human life inside of us for nine months until the child can survive on their own outside our womb. Oh yeah, and we can withstand a whole lot of pain. We are amazing at multitasking, being emotionally intelligent, and for centuries we have made sure we care for others before we care for ourselves. In the workforce, companies with female leaders do better than their all-male counterparts. There is so much awesomeness to being a woman.

So why do women experience joy when seeing another woman's pain? Why do we go in with caution when meeting another woman rather than genuinely trying to be her friend? While men have the "Bro Code" and "Man Law", where is the Code for Women?

Hollywood has capitalized on how women treat each other negatively. There is a reason *The Real Housewives of Orange County* was such a success that there are now sister cities sharing in the drama (Beverly Hills, Atlanta, New York, Potomac, etc). I have sat amidst many different groups of women talking about these shows. Other than the pure addictive qualities of these shows (I mean, I love Kandi and Kyle!), one trend I noticed among these groups was they didn't talk about the parts of the shows that highlighted the good the housewives did. Some of these housewives sponsor, lead and organize events that drive public awareness for issues women and the world face. These housewives have overcome adversity and try to affect positive change. But what does the audience focus on? The drama. Who is gossiping about whom? Who is betraying whom? The ratings don't lie. We can't blame the show because if the audience didn't like the content, it would have not made it past season one. Our priorities are out of order.

This book uses my experiences to highlight the current negative state of female relationships. I am not talking about the *mean girls* found in high school. No, no—this is a different, and bigger, problem to tackle as the problem carries into adulthood. We are enemies to each other, hence the title *Womenemies*. There is something wrong with the way women treat each other, and I want to use my experiences and those of my loved ones to demonstrate our failures and provide a solution.

The title might suggest a negative tone to this book. To the contrary—the message is a positive and hopeful one. In order to fix a problem and move forward, the problem has to be examined. Each chapter of this book examines a different problem and then takes it a step further and provides a lesson to affect positive change. This examination is part of the solution since some women might not know the effect their womenemy actions have on other women. Providing honest, real examples will hopefully shed light on the detrimental and hurtful effects these negative actions cause. The reader might think the lesson at the end of every chapter is simple and easy—and the reader would be correct. They might have even heard some of them before. There are so many simple fixes to the way women treat each other, but the trick is that people actually have to put those simple fixes into action. Why haven't we done that yet? This book hopes to reinforce how simple positive change can be.

The end result: This book unifies women by offering an outlet for women to identify with similar situations and know others are going through the same experiences. It also provides a solution—a set of guidelines to further unify and uplift each other to a better level of life.

What inspired me to write about this topic? It is said the most powerful enlightenment comes from a painful part of our lives. This was definitely true for me. I was cheated on by my fiancé when I was in my late twenties. My entire world was rocked and felt like it was crumbling. The negative communication and experience I had with the other woman was the catalyst for me to look at how women treat each other. I realized I, too, was a womenemy at times and I needed to change.

The below email was from Kayla, the "other woman" to my then fiancé. While I knew it was Kayla, she was pretending to be another woman—Rosalina. She was writing me this email almost one year after I ended things with my fiancé due to him sleeping with her for two years.

Hello Marilena,

Nice to be able to catch up with you again. From what I hear, once again you are going after my man. I know you remember me. I don't understand why you keep messing with Carter when he no longer wants to be with you. I don't know if you know but even though he moved to Miami, we still find the time to see each other. We have a past and you are not going to ruin that. I was over there with my dancing group and he sure found time to spend with me. It's obvious that he still wants to see me and be with me so I don't understand why you have to keep being in the way. No matter what I will always be here with him, so just let it go.

About a minute after reading it, my boss entered my office and saw my Mediterranean temper exposed all over my face. He told me to take a deep breath and not to write anything back to this woman without his approval. I nodded and attempted to wait to click the Send button after writing a response. However, my boss' meeting was taking too long, and I wanted to make sure I sent the email before this woman changed her email address again (it was common for her to go under fake names and emails). This was my response:

Dear Rosalina, or whatever your real name is,

I actually have no idea who Rosalina is, and therefore have never had contact with you. If you are really Kayla, who has used different emails and names in the past when trying to contact me, then I do know who you are unfortunately and I feel very sorry for you.

Either way, addressing me in the manner which you have is completely demonstrative of your character and class. Only a person who is immature and classless would talk to me the way you did. Since you obviously know who I am, then you should know that I was with Carter for 10 years, he proposed to me and we were engaged, and his family still considers me a daughter. He moved out to California to be with me when I finished law school, and only left to Miami solo because I left him.

To also refresh your memory I never retaliated or blamed you when you told me you were sleeping with my fiancé. I do find it sad when a woman who knows a man is engaged degrades herself and disrespects another woman just to be a man's mistress, or as you refer to it in your dialect—"jump off". I know from the emails between you and him that you knew who I was, and I feel sorry that your morals are that depleted for you to disrespect another woman and clearly yourself.

If this is not Kayla, and just another one of Carter's women, then you already know you are probably one of many. I don't know what history you have and I truly do not care. I will tell you one thing—know your facts before attacking an educated woman who doesn't have time for arguments without merit.

First, I have never gone after your man. He was my man and fiancé up until last July. After that date I have never contacted him to get him back. Therefore, I am not once again after your man, though I highly doubt he is your man.

Second, Carter has actually been the one trying to get me to come back. He has emailed me, texted me, and contacted my family and our friends regarding getting me back and marrying me. He loves me and always will because I was a good woman to him. And he admits fully he will always regret what he did. Just this past Saturday, he texted me to tell me he still misses me and loves me.

Third, if this is Kayla, and I really think it is, your history with Carter was meaningless. Yeah you knew him for two years, and had sex, and he met your family. But to him and all his friends you were just his chick on the side and I was the one woman he loved and wanted to marry. I will not go into comparing histories, because it is pointless—you will never have what I had with Carter. A true, honest and loving woman always prospers—remember that. And unfortunately honey, you will always be a loser unless you change your ways.

As I conclude this email, I truly hope you better yourself in life because you are leading a pretty sad existence. Obviously you are obsessed with me and my actions as you found my new email address and probably have my phone number. Unlike you who hides under different names and emails, I am here and not hiding as I have nothing to be ashamed of. I think why you contacted me is out of your own insecurities. If you didn't view me as a threat, then you wouldn't even feel the need to contact me and tell me to let go. You should be confident that Carter is only interested in you and no one else. If you truly thought Carter was only into you, you wouldn't have the need to contact me.

But, you are right about one thing—you should be threatened by me. You and everyone else knows that I was the love of Carter's life and I could have him back anytime I wanted. So when you are with him acting in sin, remember that he is probably wishing and hoping he was with me.

Goodbye.

Kayla went on to reply to me the following day, and I emailed her back with a stronger and yes, more mean response. That response can be found in the "Don't Be The Other Woman" chapter.

I will admit that referring to her as a "jump off" made me feel happy. Even throwing it in her face that the man she wanted loves me made me feel some joy. While I realized that I probably felt that way because this woman had done some things to purposefully hurt me and I was just expressing my anger, at the same time it dawned on me that I had made a miniscule step down to Kayla's level. I became a womenemy because I was getting some joy from another woman's pain.

My interaction with Kayla, girls in college, and even beyond have really made me think about how women treat each other. Prior to college, I never had such negative interactions with women. I have been blessed with extraordinary females in my life. My best friend has been in my life since I was eight months old and she has never left my side. We will call her Angel—because that is just what she is, a true divine blessing. I have also had friends since middle school and high school who have shown me the value of honesty, loyalty, and defending a loved one's honor. I never had to worry about them talking about me behind my back or sharing my very personal business with others.

As you can see, I was spoiled. So when I entered college, I thought all girls were just like the girls I grew up with. I went to a completely different state without knowing anyone on purpose. I like to meet new people and learn more about their background, culture, and viewpoint. I was lucky when I met my roommate—she had all the traits of my childhood friends (in fact she is one of my good friends still), and this furthered my perception that all women shared the same characteristics to which I had been accustomed. After a couple months at college in the cold New England weather, I came face-to-face with the harsh reality that I was terribly naïve when it came to how females treated each other.

That's when Alina entered my life. She was a year older

7

than me and had directed me to audition for a dance group when she overheard me say that I really wanted to continue with my favorite hobby—dance. I was very grateful for her advice and I started to hang out with her more often. I knew she was struggling financially, so I would sometimes buy her food or pick up the tab when we were out. I didn't think much of it because growing up, my friends and I used to fight over who could pay the bill—we never counted to the dime who owed what. Rather, we all did it out of care and love and trust that our niceness wouldn't be exploited.

Alina would confide in me about her familial and boy troubles. She would introduce me to different guys she was interested in, and I would support her. She even introduced me to my college boyfriend with whom I would fall madly in love. I really thought we were close. A couple months into our friendship during my freshman year, I realized that Alina was spreading rumors about me, trying to sleep with the guy I was dating, and overall using me for financial reasons. That shattered me, but it wasn't the last of my shocking encounters with women.

As I started to write this book almost a decade ago in a Santa Monica coffee shop, my goal was to discuss, examine, and analyze my experiences in order to provide honest, real examples and lessons that can be integrated into our daily lives in order to eradicate the existence of womenemies. But in order to eradicate the enemy, the enemy must be acknowledged. This is why I am writing.

C'mon, ladies, let's try to be more like guys in this respect and band together to help each other!

Chapter 2

Don't Share Other People's Secrets
Don't Gossip

It's unfortunate, but we have all been culprits in the respect of "spilling the beans." I am not quite sure, but a lot of females feel like they might just explode if they receive this juicy piece of information from a friend and don't share it. For those couple seconds of sharing someone's secret and seeing the expression of our captivated audience, we get a thrill like we just passed along some crucial information. Yet we are not sharing scientific or groundbreaking news. Most of the time we are just sharing some piece of gossip that has no significance to the life of our audience.

While our audience usually does not have any vested interest in the drama of others' lives, the person whose secrets are being told to a stranger is the victim here. We become womenemies to that poor female victim when we participate in gossip. To have intimate secrets shared can be analogized to someone sharing your naked photos. In fact, it is worse than that—photos are superficial, whereas intimate secrets are so sacred that the sense of violation runs deep. We need to stop this betrayal. Best rule of thumb—ask the person if you can share the information. If you think they will say no, don't even broach the subject and zip the lip. If you have the chutzpah to ask and they say no, no means NO! If Sel, Donna and Trisha had followed this advice, the below two stories wouldn't have even existed.

Following the broken engagement, I fell into a dark place where I just felt so down, I cried constantly and basically felt my life was over. I broke down to my girlfriend, Sel, so many times. I would tell her personal information about how my fiancé ran up debt, wouldn't touch me toward the end, and how I found out he was cheating. I would talk about how I was unhappy with my job and how I felt hopeless. Admittedly, my situation was not the easiest to handle—I didn't even want to handle it myself. So I couldn't blame a friend for not knowing how to deal. I wasn't prepared, though, when I attended Sel's graduation party and her colleagues and friends expressed how they knew specific details about my dark months.

I was embarrassed, felt betrayed, and wished I could erase everything. But I couldn't get that back—people knew some of the most intimate parts of my financial, sexual and emotional life. On top of that, the stories were told from Sel's point of view. Maliciously or not, some stories got muddled and facts distorted. That part of my life was mine—and I felt I should have been the only person to decide what was told and to whom it was told.

When I finally confronted Sel, all she could say was that she found it extremely hard to be my friend and she needed to vent to her friends and get advice on how to deal with me. In retrospect, as much as it would have hurt to hear that my friend couldn't be there for me during my toughest hour, I would have much preferred she walk away from me than act as my confidant and share my secrets with strangers thousands of miles away.

If people want gossip, we have enough tabloids, reality shows and talk shows to handle that demand. For commoners like me, who don't put ourselves in the public eye or hold ourselves out as a celebrity, our life stories should be our own. My experience with betrayal doesn't compare with what a college classmate of mine experienced.

Bailey was a sweet and caring girl who was going through the transition we all go through—figuring out who we are. She had plans to go to graduate school and was trying to be everyone's friend on campus. A stunning woman, but like most college girls, she carried distorted views of her beauty and struggled with insecurities. Most college guys didn't even deserve to have the privilege of taking her out on a date. A typical college story—she chose the flashy playboy. And she was happy. We, her friends, didn't know him well, but it was college, so we didn't think anything serious would culminate from the relationship.

Out of all my friends, you could have placed Bailey at the top of the list regarding who was completely against the domestic life. She didn't cook, she believed the help should clean, and she didn't want to be tied down or be called "wifey." She was all about traveling, education and going on to graduate school. She believed the man should always make more money than his wife, and when she *one day* (and that was light-years away) settled down, it would be with a kind, successful, old-school gentleman who was capable of caring for her and the rug rats (that was her term) she would birth. Needless to say, it was clear to all of us that domestic life for Bailey was at least a decade away, if not more.

My senior year in college I had a crazy, *crazy* dream that came out of nowhere—in my dream I received a phone call from Bailey. She said she was pregnant, and all of us were shocked. Of course, I forgot my dream in the morning. However, in the afternoon on my way home from class, I got a flashback of the dream and just started laughing. That reminded me to call Bailey, as I had not spoken to her in a while. I had committed the big girl sin—forsaking my girls for my new man.

I was driving a stick shift with the phone to my ear (before the laws of no talking and driving). *Ring. Ring. Ring.* I thought it was going to voicemail.

"Hello," she answered groggily. Probably hungover from Thirsty Thursday Nights.
"Hi Bailey—" I was cut off.
"Hi Mari, haven't heard from you in a hot minute."
"I know, I suck. I had to call you because I had the funniest dream about you. Dudette, you were preggos and you called me to tell me about it."

I was waiting for her to crack the hell up and say, "Girl, don't even put that *ish* into the universe." Instead I got complete silence. I looked at my phone to check that the call had not been disconnected. Nope, still there.

"Mari, I think I am pregnant." She basically whispered it—as if she said it softly, she wouldn't hear it herself. I pulled over to the side of the road. I would have caused a collision otherwise.

All I said was, "I am here for you. You need me to get a pregnancy test?" She said yes. I went to CVS and withstood the judgmental stare from the sole pharmacist who also provided me with my monthly birth control pills. I picked up two tests and rushed over to the dorms.

Positive. Twice. Yes, Bailey was pregnant. She begged me not to tell anyone. I promised and had her come over to my apartment. I was safer for her to be with—the rest of our crew lived on campus. And my removal from the crew because of my boyfriend and LSATs actually made me separated from daily college life and easier to talk to. The next day we went to Planned Parenthood and found out how far along Bailey was. One month.

Bailey had to make a decision that no one wants to make. For cultural reasons, she would be disowned by her entire family just for having premarital sex. I told her that it was her decision, and I would always be there for her. I also counseled her to not share this with many people—our university was huge, but gossip made it feel like a small village. People knew who I was and where I lived because of whom I dated. Bailey agreed and moved ahead with her choice.

The procedure occurred, and the guy, a.k.a. the father, accompanied Bailey. Her friends, including me, gave her all the support we could and things seemed fine. As law school applications came close and my relationship had its own struggles, I had become more distant from college life. Soon I found out that Bailey had started to hang out with the only two girls on campus who hated me. One of them, Donna, had been like a leech—clinging to everyone in my life because my boyfriend chose to claim me as his girl rather than her. Donna was not a happy person and was coming into my friend circle quickly. The other one, Trisha, was jealous of my friendship with her boyfriend and wanted me out of the picture.

Though I had isolated myself from the university life, out of

13

care and love I told Bailey they (Donna and Trisha) were not to be trusted. Bailey expressed her appreciation for my concern but stated that she believed Donna and Trisha had turned over a new leaf. While I wanted to believe her, my gut strongly disagreed. Unfortunately, my gut prevailed. A month later a male friend of mine approached me and asked if it was true Bailey had once been pregnant. I denied the truth, as it was not my truth to tell. Four others proceeded to inquire as to the truth of the rumor, and all four admitted the source of the gossip leak—Donna and/or Trisha.

Very soon the campus of over 18,000 undergraduates felt like a campus of 300 where half of the attendees knew of Bailey's very personal experience. Bailey was not happy and the rumor followed her through graduation. This infuriated me. The repercussions for Donna and Trisha were miniscule—at most, their already well-founded reputation of being useless gossipers was confirmed. However, the repercussions for Bailey were massive—a large community of college students were privy to a sensitive, personal, and emotional choice Bailey and her boyfriend made. The daily looks and whispers from college students were all-consuming. In addition, the risk that Bailey's family would find out and consequently disown Bailey were greater. I am grateful every day that risk never became a reality, but the sheer concept of it frightened Bailey and those who loved her. Before Donna and Trisha unzipped their lips, they did not bother to think through the consequences for the subject of their gossip.

<u>Lesson</u>: Zip The Lip And Value The Word "Confidential"

When a fellow female, or better yet, a fellow human being, tells you something personal or in confidence, zip your lip. Even if they do not preface it with "please don't tell anyone" or "this is really personal," keep it confidential. If you are unsure whether it is private information, ask the source if this is information they wish to keep private. If you are too embarrassed to ask that question, and most of the time you will be, the answer is an obvious one—keep the information confidential. The next chapter gives an example of who you should emulate—Jessica. Read on to find out why.

Chapter 3

Don't Get Mad At Women Who Don't Share Others' Secrets

In addition to zipping the lip, women need to stop becoming angry when their female friends do not share information of a third party that was divulged in confidence. A lot of women think their best friend is betraying them when their friend isn't sharing other people's information. This manner of thinking is warped. Actually, the friend who doesn't betray others' confidences is the MOST trustworthy of them all and is the least likely to betray. Think of it this way—who would you trust more to hire: (1) an employee who badmouths prior employers and shares their business models, or (2) an employee who states they will not talk about prior employers in a disparaging way or reveal their business model. Let me give you another hypothetical—who would you want to marry: (1) a person with a history of cheating on their significant others, or (2) someone who has never cheated. (Hint: everyone should be picking the second choice in both scenarios.)

Lani was a bright and beautiful woman who I had befriended in my mid-twenties. I introduced Lani to my best friend Eric at a networking mixer. Eric was coming off an emotional breakup and was not looking for anything serious. I had been friends with Eric for years but didn't know a lot about his romantic life. Forever the gentleman, Eric did not mention, hint or reference any indiscretions he may have had during his "fun and single" phase of life.

Eric's excitement for life was contagious. His good looks (chiseled features, blue-green eyes, and an eight-pack—*need I say more?*) just put the cherry on top of making him irresistible to all women. Through many mutual friends' gatherings, Eric and Lani became closer. And then one night, birthday celebratory drinks combined with sleep exhaustion (we were all at the beginning of our careers), Eric and Lani "hooked up". The morning after was fine and we all hung out. Actually, for weeks it seemed they were in agreement—keep it casual. Then the crazy Lani came out...or as Eric liked to say, "Flying monkeys came out of her head."

Lani wanted more from the relationship. Like a mathematical equation, the more Lani pushed to spend time with Eric, the fewer times Eric wanted to see her. It finally culminated with Eric saying the infamous words, "I think we are better off as friends." Those eight words are a serum for insanity for any woman—we play through our heads what we did wrong, what we could have done, should have done, what we should have worn, and the numerous calls and texts we regret sending.

Well, in the end, Lani didn't do anything wrong. After three years of pining for Eric and demonstrating her hurt and frustration to her friends, Lani was going to find out that while she could have done things differently to maintain a friendship with Eric, she couldn't have done anything to make Eric agree to a romantic relationship.

Eric called to invite me over after work – he wanted to talk to me. He wouldn't say what about. In the history of our

17

friendship this had never occurred—he always gave me a preview of anything to be discussed. The "flying monkeys" started coming out of my head—was he mad at me? Was he dying? Was he breaking up with me as a friend? Moving? WHAT?! My billable hours (yeah, I am an attorney, don't hold that against me) that day were .5 due to my cognitive energy being expended on Eric hypotheticals. In fact, I should have billed Eric for a day of lost work. I think the statute of limitations on that has run.

I got to Eric's house. He brought me a beer and talked about—no joke—how the weather had changed in Santa Monica. He went on to discuss superfluous information—the status of college football, next bar to try, and the endless hell of being a civil litigator. I could sense he was nervous so I allowed him to keep this charade up for a bit. After thirty minutes, I couldn't take it anymore. "Eric, you're killing me...TELL ME!" In the ten seconds it took him to sip his beer and then put his hand to his chest, the one thing I never fathomed he would tell me was the only thought in my mind. Six years prior, two years prior, the day before, or even three minutes prior it would have never entered my mind. But in those ten seconds, I knew it before he said it. "I'm gay."

We talked for hours and it was a conversation that only brought me closer to my already BFF. Eric was not ready, given his conservative background, to hit everyone with a public headline announcing his sexual orientation. Instead, he wished to personally tell each one of his friends. After telling a couple of us, we dared to ask the question, "You going to tell Lani?" Eric decided he wasn't ready yet, but would let Mario (a mutual friend), Jessica (another mutual friend) and me know when we could tell Lani.

Jessica, the closest to Lani, had always stood up for Lani and even questioned Eric's intentions with Lani. Having witnessed the intense pain Lani experienced from Eric's rejection over the past three years, Jessica would ask, almost beg, Eric to tell Lani in hopes that Lani could use that information as closure and move on. When Eric stated he wasn't ready, Jessica respected his decision and assured him the information was in a "vault," as it was not her news to share.

Months later, Eric expressed his decision to tell Lani. As they were not on speaking terms, Eric wanted Mario, Jessica and me to be the messengers, as he hoped this would bring some peace to Lani. We set a dinner date to break the news to Lani. Jessica could not make it due to a family emergency, but her thinking was "the sooner the better" regarding Lani knowing the information and asked Mario and me to tell her.

We went for guacamole and margaritas. On the second round of skinny margaritas, we told Lani we had to tell her something. She looked at us with confusion and exhibited trepidations about the pending subject matter. Mario just ripped off Lani's emotional Band-Aid with the following words: "Eric is gay." Lani appeared shocked but quickly masked it with a calm expression. Surprisingly, she didn't have any questions. I could see Lani entering into her protective mode—in order to divert attention from her pain, she laughed and said, "It makes sense now..."

I could see her internal pain and imagined her thoughts. *Was I that awful that I turned him gay?* Lani then proceeded to fill the silence with her jokes about how others thought Eric was in love with me, and now that my engagement was broken, Eric and I would run off together. Lani then quickly changed the topic to me and how I was coping/surviving/existing with being single after ten years in a serious relationship. My scars were still fresh, but I accepted her throwing the proverbial salt into my wounds if it meant distracting the thoughts in Lani's mind. I knew more of her thoughts and pain were to follow, but none of us foresaw to whom she was to direct her anger.

Poor unsuspecting Jessica. She was the target. Lani slowly removed herself from Jessica's life and increased the amount of time she spent with Jessica's frenemies. Side bar— frenemies are people who appear to be your friend but really talk behind your back, compete with you, and are your enemy. During those hangout sessions with the frenemies, Lani would join in on Jessica-bashing sessions. The four-year friendship, full of ups and downs, ended when Lani asked Jessica to dinner. At the dinner Lani said she didn't think she could trust Jessica since she hid Eric's secret for so long knowing it would make a difference in Lani's emotional well-being if Eric's truth had been revealed. Jessica stood by her decision to honor Eric's secret until he was ready to share it. In Jessica's eyes, this was a personal decision only Eric could make and she valued her reputation among her close friends as being trustworthy and a vault for confidential information.

I have definitely been a culprit of being a womenemy by getting mad at a loyal friend who refuses to divulge secrets. As I analyzed why I wasted energy being mad at a loyal person, I realized it is easier to place blame than deal with feelings of hurt or confusion. I definitely think due to the shocking news of Eric being gay, it was easier to blame Jessica than deal with all the confusing emotions of pining over a guy who was unattainable.

I do want to note that Lani is a very successful businesswoman now who uplifts very many women, including me. She has assisted me in my own career when I needed help, even though we had not talked in years. I say this to point out that all of us can make mistakes and become a womenemy, but that doesn't make the existence of the womenemy permanent.

<u>Lesson:</u> Value The Friend Who Keeps Things Confidential

We should all be so lucky to have a Jessica in our lives. Women, don't get mad at the Jessicas of the world who are a vault to those who share secrets with them. It is the Jessicas in this world that you can trust—when they give you their word to keep something confidential, they mean it...no matter how good or juicy the secret.

Chapter 4

Don't Be The Other Woman

Ahhhh, this chapter rings true for many as most women have been a part of this story—either as the other woman, the betrayed woman, the friend of the betrayed woman, or the friend of the other woman. But before I get on with this chapter and part two of my dealings with Kayla, I want to make the point clear—don't forget that the man broke his promise, vow, etc. Many women tend to blame the other woman and focus on her actions, then just take back the man, or worse, never confront the man about his actions. As I said in Chapter 1, "*I do find it sad when a woman who knows a man is engaged degrades herself and disrespects another woman just to be a man's mistress...*", but in the end it is the man who is IN the relationship and decided to disrespect it. What each woman wants to do with her relationship is her prerogative, I am just saying that you should make sure you don't distract yourself from the man's betrayal by focusing on the other woman.

The blame goes 100 percent to the man, but we become womenemies to each other when we knowingly engage in relations with a married/otherwise taken man; when we don't tell our friends they are being cheated on; and when we don't tell our friend to stop being the other woman.

In my situation, I chose to leave my fiancé as the betrayal

was too deep for any recovery. While I focused on his betrayal, I did find myself getting very angry at Kayla for being the other woman to a man she knew was engaged. But I kept telling myself, even when I spoke to her on the phone when I first found out, that the main person to blame was the person who I thought was the love of my life. It wasn't until a year later when Kayla had the audacity to email me to tell me to back off *her* man that I exploded. I mean, I didn't do anything mean to her or harass her after I found out she slept with my fiancé for two years knowing we were engaged and even seeing my photos on his nightstand. But to accuse me of trying to steal *her* man? Oh helllllllll noooo. In chapter one you saw my response to her emailing me to stay away. As promised, here was her response to my email:

You can continue to paint your story as pretty as you want to. You know that the relationship you had was not as true and honest as you may have thought it was or he wouldn't have ended up with me. Carter never had a gun to his head and he enjoyed it very well. He will always be Carter and if it's not with me it will be with someone else. I'm sure that as the smart and educated woman you are you know that to be fact.

Have a nice life!!!

Was I angry? YES. Was I going to respond? HELL YES. Did my dear friend want to respond on my behalf and call Kayla a two-cent jar that holds male semen (in her exact words, a "___ jar"—you can fill in the bad word)? Yup. Side note: I am blessed - I have protective friends. While I didn't call her a ___ jar, I did reply with the following:

Obviously you didn't understand my last email. Maybe try using a dictionary next time to understand the big words,

23

sweetie. Also, a person either writes a story or paints a picture—but I have never heard of what you described as painting a story! hahaha. I think you should probably go back to school or sue the education system for how you turned out.

You are right, I am a very educated woman. And I know when it is worthless to continue to argue with an uneducated and completely ignorant person who has no meaning in life. My life fortunately is full of love, happiness and respect. So after this email I am done with you.

I will not defend myself to you. I know what Carter and I had, and that is all that matters. I also know you were the biggest mistake of his life. If you are truly with him, then you shouldn't care about all that. You should know in your heart he only wants you. But alas, you are a delusional waste of space. As someone who ended up with you would not write the below email. That email can be summed up in three easy words for you to understand—he hates you. I will have a wonderful life and bright future. Unfortunately, you will always just be the other woman to anyone in your life—the woman a man will defile but never propose to as you aren't worth a $5 ring pop. By the way "defile" is under the "d" section of the dictionary— just wanted to save you some time looking it up.

I suggest next time you want to engage in a debate with a woman of my stature and pedigree—don't. Keep your mouth closed as you should have kept your legs closed in life. I hope you find Jesus. I have cc'd Carter on this email. Maybe if he ever decides to speak to you again he can explain it in a way which someone with your education level (or lack thereof) would understand.

Enjoy reading the below email again—I certainly did. Stop contacting me. Deuces.

Yes, I ended with "Deuces." Super corny, but I had listened to the Chris Brown song too many times. The email I referenced from Carter to Kayla is nothing worth pasting into this book, as it contained a bunch of swear words and ended with "F***in' hate you." Ouch for Kayla. My immature side smiled.

That was the last I heard from Kayla. But I will say, looking back I just shouldn't have responded. I didn't owe her the time I took from my day to write those mean things. Even though it felt good to be mean to someone who completely disrespected me, and who was my womenemy, if my daughter or dear friend were ever in the same position as me, I would just tell them to walk away and not respond.

When Your Friend Is The Other Woman

Lena was a dear friend with whom I shared ten years of friendship. Lena was my confident, beautiful, loves-to-dance partner in crime on the dance floor. Following college Lena was single, as she had outgrown her high school boyfriend. We all did celebratory dances—she deserved so much better. A new single Lena, she finally saw the attention from men that she never noticed. And she liked it—I mean, who wouldn't?

I was living in another state than Lena and living with my then fiancé. Lena would come to visit us quite frequently along with a close college friend, Todd. Todd was actually my friend first but quickly established a bond with my then fiancé. Todd and Lena knew each other for years and we all would laugh and hang out as friends. There was never a connection between the two—I even tried to make the connection once and was told a solid "no" by Lena. So I put the overbearing Greekness that ran through my blood aside and respected her wishes.

One Labor Day weekend, Lena and Todd came and visited us. Todd was dating people, or as they commonly say on the East Coast, "talking to people", but nothing serious or exclusive. I had mentioned that I wanted to set up Todd with my amazing friend Charmaine, and there was a perfect opportunity during the holiday weekend. Todd was open to it and Lena seemed happy for the set-up attempt, or so I thought. After dinner one night, we all went out for drinks, and Charmaine pulled me aside and asked if Lena liked Todd or if she had ever dated Todd. I immediately said no and followed up by asking why that even came to Charmaine's mind. Charmaine explained that she felt a certain overprotectiveness or assertion of boundaries from Lena. I couldn't say anything, as most of the day I was cooking and didn't observe everyone socializing. I told Charmaine I would keep a closer eye on the matter and let her know.

The following day at 11 p.m., my question was answered. We were all a bit tipsy at a night club. Lena and I snuck away to the restroom, both to pee and to have girl talk away from the boys. Before I could even say anything, Lena blurted, "I want to kiss Todd tonight." I was shocked but happy—I had wanted them to get together for years. I asked her what had changed, since she always said no to my suggestions in the past. Lena said she just started to see him in a different light. I blindly accepted that. As a good friend, I told Charmaine her observations about Lena were correct, and unfortunately I couldn't set her up with Todd anymore. Charmaine was incredibly cool and understanding—and if you saw Charmaine (gorgeous) and spoke to her (extremely intelligent, kind, and genuine), you would understand that a lack of potential suitors was not her problem.

What I didn't think of until I wrote this chapter was how Lena's action of wanting Todd only when another woman could potentially date him was a blueprint of who she would eventually become—the Other Woman.

Lena and Todd started to date after that Labor Day weekend. Lena went in with eyes wide open, fully knowing she was not the only woman Todd was dating. Lena was fine with that, as she was sure the foundation of friendship she built with Todd would eventually influence him to choose her as his one and only. As the months went on, it got more serious from Lena's perspective. While my friendship with Todd was longer than that with Lena, I felt a sisterhood allegiance to Lena. Plus, given the fact that Todd would dismiss our friendship at times for his friendship with my then fiancé, I didn't mind backing off from my friendship with Todd. I finally worked up the courage to ask Lena if she and Todd were exclusive. Apparently, it had taken her months as well to build up the courage to tell me something—Todd had been dating another girl longer and it seemed serious, but Todd also wanted to continue dating Lena. "It is complicated." That was her explanation. What does that really mean? Translation: *I am the other woman and while I know I should leave him, I believe the bond is so strong that I will stick it out so he leaves his girlfriend and comes to me.*

A wise woman, ironically Charmaine's mom, once told me, "You can never start a healthy relationship off of someone else's unhappiness." I wish I had passed on those words of wisdom right then and there to Lena. Instead, I played the supportive friend and believed in Lena and Todd's love. I was a total Pollyanna.

A year passed with no change in Lena's "situation." There was a change in mine—I had left my fiancé and broken off the engagement when I heard from the other woman. Lena was there for me—calling, texting, even coming to visit. I changed states, got a new job, and seemed on the outside to be progressing. But the pain of being cheated on was deep. Lena seemed to be supportive, at first.

As the months went on, she distanced herself, as my pain was too much for her because she was also dealing with her own "situation." Translation: Todd was still with his girlfriend, who he claimed in public, yet Lena was still sleeping with him and pursuing a relationship with him. When Lena did call, she would call me crying and I told her I had no more advice to give other than that she had to move on. But only she could do it.

I sent my friends the email exchange I had with Kayla, the other woman in my situation. They found my jabs toward her hilarious and they read it out loud to their friends for amusement. It was even used for entertainment at a bachelorette party. Lena told me that as she read it, she felt bad. She knew she was the other woman, and seeing my anger in writing made her feel like an idiot. A breakthrough! Well, so I thought. I thought the final breakup with Todd was coming, but it never came from her end.

The opposite of what I expected after she read the letter happened. She moved from depression and tears to anger, bitterness, and rage. But not toward Todd—toward his girlfriend! Lena would say, "What is she, dumb or something? She doesn't know he is cheating? She just needs to go away!" While I tried to separate my painful experience from Lena's situation, when she said things like that I would work hard to refrain myself from swearing at her. Instead I would try to explain that blaming the girlfriend is not right, she had done nothing to Lena and might be so in love with Todd that she is blind. It was unfair to be mean to the girlfriend. "Maybe I shouldn't talk to you about this, it's too close to home," Lena replied. No $&*#, Sherlock. Way to deflect.

My ultimate breaking point was when Todd told Lena he couldn't break up with his girlfriend because there was a possibility she had cancer, and he wanted to stay by her side through it. "That bitch. She is lying! This is so unfair!" That was the selfish response from Lena. My stomach was in knots. Here was my one of my so-called best friends being utterly horrible to a woman who: (1) had done nothing to Lena, (2) might have cancer, and (3) was the victim of Lena and Todd's affair.

I couldn't hold back. "Lena, that is enough. This woman might have cancer and you are making this about you." That was the last we ever talked about Todd and Lena's "situation."

Shortly thereafter I found out Lena also had known my ex was cheating on me and did nothing. I was done with her. She continued to be Todd's side piece for a while. I found out later that he finally broke up with his girlfriend and promoted Lena to his official girlfriend. But Charmaine's mom's message stating that you can't build something off another's pain echoed in my head. So true. I later was told that one time, when Lena and Todd were entering a restaurant, they saw Todd's ex. Lena decided to stay outside while Todd went to say hello. Why did Lena stay outside? The ex knew Lena was the other woman. I guess the shame of being the side piece stays with someone for a lifetime.

Whatever happened with Todd and Lena? They dated for many years. Lena even moved in with him for a while when he was in graduate school. Todd and I were distanced because Lena didn't like me, and I understood that put him in an awkward situation. Still hurt, though.

The last couple months of their relationship was when Todd reconnected with me. I had just reached out to wish him well in his studies and ask if he needed me to ask friends for help with his thesis. I made a conscious effort not to bring up Lena, as Todd knew we weren't friends anymore and I didn't want that to ruin the friendship that Todd and I were trying to rebuild. I did say I knew how graduate school is stressful and how he needs to be surrounded by people who love and support him and make his life easier. That was all it took—the floodgates opened.

Todd proceeded to tell me about the emotionally abusive relationship he was in—the pressure for him to marry Lena, the multiple times she reminded him of everything she does for him, the pressure to go out more, and the anger toward his dedication to school. I did start with the disclaimer that Lena was not my favorite person, but with that said, objectively Todd needed to find a way to not have stress during school, and if he wanted to make it work, he needed to communicate with Lena and work it out. I never said to break up or anything. Everyone's relationship is private and it is up to them to make that decision.

Was I hoping he left her? Hell yes! Let me clarify why I felt this way. It was not because I wished her pain at all. It was because I didn't want to see my friend Todd in an unhealthy relationship.

When I got engaged to my now husband, I told Todd and he was so happy for me. A true friend. When I returned from London, the city where I got engaged, I had a talk with Todd. He expressed his continued stress and the fact that his mom and family didn't like to see him in his current state. I finally had to say it—"Todd, if you have tried everything, you need to find a way to make yourself happy, and while in school you need to only surround yourself with people who support you and do not cause you stress." That was the most direct I could be. He told me Lena would constantly yell at him regarding them not being engaged, how his work and school took up all his time, and how they didn't have time for fun. I knew in the past they had broken up and gotten back together. Even upon hearing this, I just stated he had to find what makes him happy, and it was up to him to determine if Lena was part of what made him happy.

Two days later I got a text from Todd. He had done it. He broke up with Lena. He thanked me for my help. I quickly responded it was all his decision, I had no part. Todd knew I had my own problems with Lena, but I always made it clear I would respect her as his girlfriend and his wife, if they got to that point. I even had given him a plus one so he could bring her to my wedding.

Here is the ironic part. Want to know the argument that was the final straw for Todd? Lena found out I was engaged. She came home and told Todd, and his reaction was that it was great news. Lena asked Todd if he had already heard my great news, and he told the truth—I had texted him when it happened. The room got silent as they ate dinner. Then her calculated statement broke the silence, "Well, she isn't invited to your graduation." While Todd didn't agree with Lena's treatment of me in the past, he always let things go and moved forward. But this he could not. For one, *his* graduation was about *him*, and all his loved ones needed to put their differences aside for *his* day. Second, I was the friend who had provided emotional and academic support during the pre-application conversations and interviews, grad school applications, and during his scholastic career. It wasn't Lena's place to take away a person who genuinely cared for Todd. The verbal fight escalated to physical when Lena bent Todd's finger backwards. Todd, not wanting to verbally react in any rage, left the house. The next day he broke things off and gave her two weeks to move out of his house.

Lena's relationship, which started off another woman's pain, ended painfully for Lena. A friend pointed out the irony of it all—Lena wanted a ring so much, and one of the people she hated most in the world, aka me, had already been proposed to twice. I laughed. It felt good to have that "one-up" on a woman who had caused me so much pain. I remembered Charmaine's mom's lesson and quickly stopped my joy over a situation I knew caused Lena so much pain. I do apologize for being happy over her pain, and while I do not talk to Lena anymore, I wish her only the best in life. Losing a man is tough, and I will not be a person who adds to or takes joy in that pain.

When Your Friend Is Being Cheated On

The answer is simple: You tell her! Doesn't matter if she never talks to you again. If you love your friend unconditionally, you tell her ASAP, and at least you can know you did everything in your power to protect your friend. A close friend of mine knew I was being cheated on, and I will say, finding that out she didn't even try to tell me and just helped plan my engagement party knowing of his infidelity hurt me, as it was a deep betrayal. You can't come back from that.

I too have been a womenemy in that I didn't tell my friend who was being cheated on. I look back at a situation from college. A girl I started to become friends with went to study abroad. I overheard that her boyfriend had spent most of the night in another girl's room. I didn't know if there was a party or not, but I knew it was a situation which would cause my friend a great amount of hurt. Because I was just becoming friends with the girl, I kept my mouth shut since I didn't see it myself. That was my cowardly excuse to avoid the situation. Looking back, even though that relationship ended in a breakup, I wish I had told her so I could have saved her more months of being in an unhealthy relationship. For that, I apologize.

Lesson: Avoid Being The Other Woman And Counsel Others To Do The Same

Being the other woman never ends well. Even if you end up with the guy, something will get in the way—guilt, the family he left behind, your friends, or karma. Therefore, the lesson is simple—if your friend is being cheated on, tell her. If your friend is the other woman, do your best to communicate to her why she should stop. If you are the other woman, stop the relationship with the man immediately. You are hurting yourself and another woman. In a sense you are a double womenemy.

Chapter 5

Don't Be Another Woman's Cause Of Stress In The Workplace

We as a gender already make less than men on average. There have been tons of inspirational protests for women's rights recently because of the elected president of the US. It was great to see women rally all over the nation and globe. However, there is a fundamental problem that has not been addressed—we band together to compete with men, however, when we compete with each other it is not healthy competition. It is mean, catty, and sometimes psychologically damaging. As a gender, we are the champions of fake smiles and passive-aggressive remarks. I even catch myself now as I write this— why did I mention women competing against each other? We need to collaborate, not compete. But if there are instances when competition is necessary, we should channel our inner Michelle Obama and stay classy, gracious, and refined.

One of the worst examples of womenemies is in the workforce. I will say that it is quite rampant in the legal industry, but you can find it anywhere. Instead of lifting each other up, we become womenemies. Yes, some can blame history, stating that the patriarchal society made it so there were only a finite amount of spots at the top of companies for women, so women had to compete for those few spots. Well, I call BS on that today. There is no reason to halt or bring down one woman's career to get ahead in your own career. Why do women get angrier when they know a woman in the workforce makes $10,000 more than them but the same woman won't get mad when a man makes $30,000 more than them in the same position?

We need to stop comparing ourselves only to women and we need to stop the jealousy. Men prey on this competition and pit women against each other in the workforce, and women play right into it! We need to uplift each other and realize the more women at the table, the better the place of employment performs. As I have previously mentioned, there are stats that show that companies who have women in leadership roles do better than the companies run by only men. It should never be *why is she at that level and not me*? But rather, it should be *how can I get to that level so there are two women at the table*?

I had a severe breakdown from stress due to a womenemy in the workforce. The work, while overly abundant, wasn't the root. The root was one woman who gossiped, made it evident she didn't like me, and tried to do my job. Every day I walked into work, I had pain in my chest. There was constant negativity. I hope this story sheds light on the ramifications of unhealthy competitiveness, cattiness, or just plain meanness toward another woman in the workforce.

Years ago, I was sitting in an airport waiting for my flight to Greece, drinking wine and just being happy to be away from the "witch". I would have used another word prior to this book, specifically the B word, but I am trying to refrain from using that, as I would be demeaning another woman with that word, and therefore, I would be a womenemy.

Asa was the "witch". Before working together, I knew her

from a prior job at another company. I knew the company she worked for and admired it for how it promoted and kept many women in management and executive roles. I loved whenever I had a chance to work with her employer. At a networking event, we were discussing career paths at our respective companies, and Asa stated how hard it was to move up in her current company. She was wondering how one would move up. From one career woman to another, I offered some advice, as she had stated she only had been in her role for one year. My advice was to learn her current role inside and out, then cross-train in her current role, so when there was an opportunity for growth, she would be prepared.

As I finished up the last couple months of my job at the time, I noticed a change in Asa whenever I was at events. She portrayed an air that she was above everyone. I was disappointed as I knew Asa was a smart, capable woman who didn't need to act in that manner.

Years later I started a new role at a new company. I was super excited except for one aspect—a big chunk of my job involved partnering with Asa. Asa was best friends with Betty, another colleague in a different department. Betty didn't like me from a couple incidents in a prior job when I had to confront her regarding her gossiping tendencies. I had moved on as it had been years since I had seen Betty, but apparently Betty had not. I didn't let that bother me too much, as I knew I could be professional and our paths would not cross much.

As far as Asa was concerned, I told myself all I could do was be professional, courteous, and just do the work. Do not get involved in drama. That was the hope. And my hope was that Betty's feelings toward me would not affect how Asa felt about me or treated me.

My first day my schedule commanded I meet Asa in the lobby at 9 a.m., and she would give me a tour of the office and introduce me to everyone. I arrived at 8:55 a.m. No Asa. 9 a.m., no Asa. The assistant manager kindly offered to show me around. I said I would love to, but would wait for Asa. At 9:10 a.m., Asa was still not there. My boss concluded her morning meeting and I met with her in another room as we waited for Asa. When Asa arrived, she hugged my boss and provided me a subtly cold hug. Only I could tell the difference but just kept it to myself. Hopefully she would warm up.

During the day, there was a time I was left alone with Asa. *Oh boy, will this be awkward?* I thought. "Well, as you got married, I basically got divorced." Asa explained she and her fiancé broke up in the years since we last saw each other. How to respond to that? "I'm sorry" was all I could say. Yup, it was the start of an awkward working relationship.

I would take awkward over witchy. Yup, I was staying positive. Well, the Pollyanna in me quickly started to see the awkwardness fade away and the passive-aggressive, toxic environment develop. In just eight months, Asa tried to give me orders, she tried to do my job, she kept me off email chains, and she lied. Oh, did she lie. Lied about why she was late, lied about attending important events, and lied about how she helped introduce me to clients.

Right before my vacation to visit my family in Greece, I had my first big presentation in my new role. I had worked with Tatiana, a phenomenal manager who trained me in learning her market, helped me gather the pertinent information for the presentation, and collaborated with me to present the information to senior management. My boss, Clara, also had my back and helped me tweak my presentation to best appeal to senior management. I was lucky to have a boss and a colleague who had my back and wanted me to shine.

Well, amid a supportive audience, in walked Asa to the presentation, and the negative energy was palpable. Never mind that she looked upset during the whole presentation, made catty comments like "did you just let that slip through cracks?", or got up while I was speaking to walk across room and put her lipstick on in front of everyone. What got me was when she started whispering during my presentation. I had it! I stopped the presentation and just waited until she was done. Yes, I felt like a schoolteacher. Yes, it felt good to point out to the room how disrespectful she was being. Like I said, I had it!

While in Greece I told my father, who I frequently went to for advice, that I couldn't take much more of the toxic environment. Working in every other aspect of my job, I was partnered with female managers who were uplifting, collaborative, and had genuine care for others. That was the core reason I loved my job. But I admit I let Asa get under my skin—I was bothered that I was working harder, was a nicer person, and I was making less than her. It bothered me that she was disrespectful in her conversations with her team. It bothered me that I had to find a way to partner with someone who differed from me so much on a moral (and morale) level.

My father's advice? "When you have to work with that woman, just laugh inside of you and treat every day as it is your last at the company. Be kind, be thoughtful, work hard, and then leave on time. Do not let her bring your spirit down." Good advice. I said I would try.

I came back from a short vacation refreshed and hopeful that I could maybe infuse positivity into my relationship with

Asa just so at least we were cordial. That hope was eviscerated on my first day back. You know that feeling when you walk into a room or stand by someone and your chest tightens and you feel this negative energy? Well, that feeling was amplified every time I was around Asa. We Greeks believe in the evil eye, a sort of negative energy transferred from people who are either jealous or have bad sentiments toward you. And every day I was around Asa, I felt that evil eyeness aimed right at me. I only wished the old village Greek grandmas were close so they could do the ritual that casts the evil eye spell away!

While I dealt with Asa on a very regular basis, which exposed me to a lot of negativity, I was grateful for a boss and other coworkers who were supportive and helped me learn and progress in my career. But when it came to Asa, my anger and exhaustion in dealing with her was hard to put into words. I didn't recognize myself when I tried to coherently relay to a career mentor of mine all the ways in which Asa created a toxic environment for me. "Tried" being the operative word, as all I did was cry. I even had printed out notes and had rehearsed it. I never let Asa see tears come from my eyes, but when explaining to my mentor, I started to cry. I apologized, as I knew that was unprofessional. And what did my mentor do? She said, "That's okay. You are angry. This is normal." That put me at ease more than anything as my career mentor was someone who I never had worked with but always admired how she handled and interpreted situations. But still the fact that Asa brought me to tears, albeit angry ones, really bothered me. It was disgusting.

Even more disgusting was the one time I received an apology from Asa, she immediately asked me whether I was going to tell my boss or if she could. She was more eager to alert my boss to the fact that she had apologized than to check to see if I was okay. Insincerity at its best!

My professional maturity was tested on a day I was awaiting an important call from my family regarding my grandmother's health. I had just finished an unproductive meeting with Asa where I had asked if she had the notes prepped and documents I requested via email a week ago. Her response? She didn't even remember my email. Then she asked if I was at a certain conference and I said, "Asa, I was sitting right next to you." I giggled as I would have with any friend of mine, as that was a serious "*duh*" moment.

The meeting ended. I went back to my desk thinking of all the tasks I needed to complete before I headed out to take the call regarding my grandmother. Asa came back to my desk and asked if I could come back to her office for a moment. I obliged and took my notepad. As she walked away, she said that I didn't need to bring a notepad. *Uh oh*, I thought. Upon entering her office and sitting down, Asa said, "I have felt some tension from you since we started working together." She wanted to know what was going on.

I had two choices: (1) be completely honest and say that I knew she didn't like me, that she was condescending in emails and verbally, and that she never voiced her appreciation or worked as a team; or (2) take the high road that might lead to a productive (or semi productive) future relationship. I decided to take the latter approach.

"Asa, I am constantly wanting to improve myself, so please give me examples of when I have caused you tension so I can work on it," is how I replied. Asa had nothing to say to that. She said she couldn't give an example. She asked if I had an example of the tension and I held back and only gave two.

41

Giving too many would have been counterproductive.

Rather than apologizing, she just tried to defend herself. To diffuse the situation, I just mentioned that since joining I had worked really hard, had to make all my own introductions (I left out the fact that she failed to introduce me at all), and I just hustled to try to learn everything in my new role. Asa mentioned that she appreciated my work ethic and I was doing a fantastic job. She asked that we start fresh. I said of course. That ended it. I went back to my desk and moved on. Did a miracle happen and did she change? Nope! But I had the victory in choosing to be the bigger person.

From that day on I made a pact that all I could do was my best to bring my positive, genuine self to work every day and give 100 percent. I knew I needed to make a concerted effort to avoid stooping to Asa's level by trying to do things to get under her skin. I knew that would never make me feel better and it would just mean I would be acting catty, even if justified. Some days I did fail and I fought back when my moral compass went haywire and I chose not to rise above. Most of the time, I refrained from being the womenemy, as I would never want to make anyone feel the way I felt in the workplace due to Asa's actions.

The end result? I moved on from that career. Do I hold anger toward Asa? No. More sympathy, as I know for someone to treat others in a poor manner means she must be unhappy. I truly wish her happiness, and I hope she finds a way to uplift others, just like the examples I provide you below of the awesome women who have impacted me.

Lesson: **Support And Uplift Your Female Colleagues**

On the flip side, when a female mentor, boss, or colleague takes the time to uplift you, it changes your world. I have been blessed with the boss, mentor, and colleagues I described above who uplifted me, trained me, and mentored me to excel in my career. Also, for almost four years I was fortunate to be trained, counseled, and mentored by Sharon, a woman who has worked all over the country for the same company and who oozes integrity and has her team's best interest always as a priority. She listened to my interests, encouraged me to take risks, made sure I shined to upper management, and was always direct with me. She gave me tough love at times too, but because of her transparency I knew it always came from a place of care and desire for me to succeed. She embodied #BossGoals.

Then there's also Tatiana, who I described in this chapter. She always did her best to show me daily unconditional support and partnership. She taught me communication and efficiency techniques as well as the importance of putting family life (the REAL LIFE) first. I am forever indebted to Tatiana as well. #Womanrolemodel

Support Women Coming Back To Work

Embracing women when they return from a leave of absence is necessary and can have a big impact on the woman returning back to work. While I was on maternity leave, Lorena, my colleague, took over my work and oversaw my markets. The fear of losing one's job is common among women out on maternity leave. Because of Lorena's genuine care to support me and her open communication, I never felt as if she was trying to take my job. In fact, when I came back to work, Lorena and my whole team showered me with love and told me how happy they were to have me back. I was very blessed to have that support. #Supportworkingmamas

Support The New Woman

Also, when a woman starts a new job it is equally necessary that she feels supported. "What if no one likes me?" "What if others question why the company hired me?" These are common questions people ask when starting a job, and may I add I believe women probably ask them more, as they are more prone to suffering from imposter syndrome. Having a coworker embrace and welcome the new female colleague brings a sense of community and provides the new hire with confidence that they are accepted. When I recently started my current job as the vice president of a law firm, I didn't know anyone except the partner and senior attorney. The office manager, Sarah, immediately embraced me, showed me the ropes, and made me feel comfortable to ask as many questions as I needed. From time to time, she would even stop by to say I was doing a great job. I am very hard on myself, and when starting a new job and working so hard, a fear is that maybe no one is seeing that hard work and the results. Sarah didn't wait for me to ask her, she took it upon herself to uplift me and give me positive feedback. Being supportive and welcoming to the new female colleague, as Sarah did, helps eliminate doubtful thoughts so the only focus of the new colleague is to get better every day at her job. #TrueWelcome #TrueSupporter

Support The Woman Who Tries Something New

That support should funnel to women who want to start their own business. "Should you really start your own business when you have a child?" "Shouldn't your focus be your family?" Why can't women have both? Just because a woman loves her career and wants to start something on her own doesn't mean her family doesn't come first. My dear friends Callie and Dora have always supported me whenever I tried to do something on my own, whether that be a blog, a side hustle, or a creative idea. Even writing this book, Dora offered to create a website and Callie offered to market it on social media. Most importantly, Dora and Callie saw how much joy I had when writing or talking about this book, and they constantly pushed and reminded me to believe in myself and publish this book. #UnconditionalSupport #FriendsWhoPushYou

Stand Up For Your Fellow Female Colleague

Finally, it is important to stand up for your fellow colleague when she is not being treated fairly. When I was a law clerk there was Ashley, a female senior attorney, who took me under her wing, spent hours working with me to improve my writing, and stood up for me when I was hazed by a lower level female attorney. Ashley could have just ignored me, given me assignments, and continued to up her billable hours. Instead, she took the time to teach me how to be a better writer, attorney, and overall professional. She is a dear friend to me now and I admire how she has amounted so much success without losing her ethics and compassion. #SheisaBoss

I am very lucky and proud of the law firm I work for, as there is daily evidence of uplifting and supporting women and everyone in general. To keep this culture going, I remind myself daily to ensure everyone, not just women, are supported the way Sharon, Tatiana, Lorena, Sarah, and Ashley have supported me.

Chapter 6

Don't Be A Mother/Monster-In-Law

Many stories, books, and even movies have been made shedding light on women's troubling, stressful, and frequently negative relationships with their mothers-in-law. We all know there is a special bond between mothers and their sons, and of course the mothers will be protective of their sons, especially when it comes down to with whom the son will be spending the rest of his life. But why do so many mothers take it a step further and just become plain mean and destructive to some good women?

To remedy this, we women need to fight the natural urge to dislike the woman our son will bring home. Note, this urge is deeply ingrained in us. Even before the woman or girl is in the picture, we don't want to like them. Shoot, my son was still in my belly and the thought of another woman taking him away made my mama bear self grimace. It makes sense—we feel that the woman will be our replacement as the person who takes care of our son. But just like with careers, why does there have to be just one woman who takes care of someone? Why does the marriage to a woman mean the mom is not needed? There is room for both women, in different capacities, of course. What we need to do is look at the possibility of a daughter-in-law as the opportunity to add one more strong, caring, and loving woman to the family who will make our son happy and therefore make us happy. And note: when we accept the daughter-in-law, the risk of losing our son decreases greatly, as the better the relationship between mother and daughter-in-law, the higher the chances of many voluntary family get-togethers. I wish my mother-in-law understood this lesson.

I never thought I would have a problem with my mother-in-law. My whole life, my friends' parents loved me. The mothers of two of my ex-boyfriends still adore me to this day. So when I started dating my now husband, I didn't think his mother would be an obstacle. My husband, a Greek just like me, had never had a serious relationship with a Greek. In fact, his ex was American and Jewish—in the Greek Orthodox community, those are two undesirable facts (I don't believe in it, but that is how it is). Not because they are antisemitic, but because they want Greeks marrying within their own ethnicity and religion. I was Greek, Greek Orthodox, family oriented, socially fluent in Greek, knew how to cook and loved to Greek dance. What Greek mother wouldn't love me? I know, I was cocky.

When she first found out her son was dating a Greek, my mother-in-law, Fotini, was thrilled. I had spoken to her a couple times on the phone and she seemed wonderful. The summer after Vasilis (my husband) and I started dating, I was vacationing with my grandparents in Greece. Fotini called my grandparents' summer house at 9 a.m. and spoke with my grandma. After returning home from being at a bar until 5 a.m., a typical Greek summer, I was still sound asleep. When I awoke my grandmother told me Fotini had phoned. I was thoroughly confused, as I had never given Fotini the phone number of my summer home, and I was quite shocked to hear that she decided to have a full-blown conversation with my grandmother.

At that point, Vasilis and I had only been dating a couple months. The reason for the call seemed innocent—she wanted to send cookies for me to bring home to her son, who was still in the States. My grandmother completely understood. That was fine and all, but the intrusion into my life, asking my grandmother questions about my life, and calling without my permission bothered me. When I called Vasilis, I asked him why she had my number. He stated he only gave his mother the phone number for emergency purposes and he specifically asked she not call, especially in the morning. The whole situation seemed innocent, but something bothered me. All I could think was Fotini seemed very forward.

Looking back on that unpermitted phone call situation, or as I like to call it, "telephonegate", I would be so lucky for that to be the only strife I experienced with Fotini. Pushy women I can deal with; I mean, I am Greek after all. Mean and insensitive I cannot.

Fast-forward a year and a half after telephonegate, Vasilis and I were engaged. We traveled to Greece during the summer to scout wedding venue locations. Also, I had never met his side of the family, so we planned to visit and his mother offered to cook us an engagement dinner. Fotini is a fantastic chef so we were excited and grateful. As I left for Tyrnavos, a small city by Larissa in the center of Greece, my grandmother and aunt warned me that the women of Tyrnavos were tough and extremely proper and to be on my best behavior. Before arriving in Tyrnavos, we made a stop to Vasilis' grandmother's house. She was so sweet and offered us a lot of food, which my father and Vasilis both accepted in large portions. I felt the love and Greek hospitality.

Vasilis and I looked at our watches and I mentioned it was 4 p.m. We decided to go see his mother before the dinner that evening. When we arrived, prior to even being hugged, we were scolded for coming so late as she had prepared lunch. Even when we mentioned we ate at her mother's, she forcefully sat us down and served us food. I did receive a hug though, so I thought maybe it wasn't going to be too bad.

After our second lunch, I asked Fotini what I could do to help. She looked me up and down in disapproval of my shorts and tank top, and told me I could go shower and change. That didn't sit well with my father, but I gave him a look begging him not to cause a commotion. I obliged, showered, and changed into a nice, long—let's not forget appropriate—dress.

Fotini had prepared multiple courses and the dinner went very well. I was thankful. At the end of the dinner, as dessert was being prepared, I caught a glimpse of the control Fotini had over her family. You see, Tyrnavos was a small town in the center of Greece close to the mountains. In the summer, there was extreme heat and no sea breeze to combat it. In Fotini's apartment, which took up the entire floor, all the balcony doors were open, however they did not welcome in a breeze, but rather the stale heat. Sweat dripped down my chest to my stomach, and then to my legs under my dress. Others were victim to the same symptoms. My father, being ever so polite, suggested to Fotini that if she shut all the balcony doors and the windows throughout the house, the air conditioner could probably circulate the cold air. Fotini responded with a "no" and commented that keeping the doors open helped the air conditioner "cut the air" and keep us cool. Whatever that meant. Vasilis' youngest brother comprehended the confused look on both my father's face and mine. He followed up with saying, "Don't bother, it won't change anything." The fact that her family and visitors thought her notion was crazy but just went along with it demonstrated that they'd rather deal with the sweltering heat than argue with Fotini. Now that is power!

The dinner ended and the guests left. After the "eating to please my in-laws" marathon day, my father and I could barely speak. Fotini didn't protest when I started to clean—she intended to put me to work. I obliged. Bedtime arrived and my father got the only room with its own air conditioner. Lucky man. Fotini insisted Vasilis and I sleep in her room. I insisted we sleep on the couch—I didn't want to inconvenience her. Truthfully, sleeping in her bed seemed weird and also, her wedding photo was right there on the vanity table. She had been divorced for almost ten years, yet wore her wedding ring and kept her wedding photo out. I didn't want to sleep in a room with that sense of alternate reality. But guess who won the argument? Fotini.

We kept the door wide open. I didn't even want the illusion that any hanky-panky was occurring in my soon-to-be mother-in-law's bed. As I was searching for my nightgown, Fotini entered with another present for me. She had given me earrings earlier that day as well as a set of towels, so I was not expecting another present. Well, Fotini saved the best for last—a nightgown for me to wear that evening. It was blue with white polka dots and it went down to my knees. Oh yeah, one more thing—it was not cotton or anything breathable! It was this material that just trapped in all the heat and sweat. *I must be getting hazed*, I thought. *Must be.*

I woke up in the middle of the night soaked in my own sweat. I felt my bones burning from the inside and there was no fan in Fotini's room. I was so angry I pinched Vasilis in order to wake him up. "Go tell your mom to shut the balcony doors and the windows in this house! I cannot take this heat," I whisper-screamed. Vasilis said she wouldn't, it was no use. Well I told him to figure something out, as I was going crazy. Vasilis went to the bathroom and brought me a towel drenched in ice-cold water. I put it all over my body, took off my nightgown, and wrapped myself in a sheet. Still hot, I felt a little bit better, enough to fall asleep. As I drifted off to sleep, I saw a face staring in from the hallway—Fotini's. While creepy, I couldn't fight or try anymore, it was what it was.

Glorious morning arrived and it was time to pack up. Even though I slept only three hours, I had a huge smile on my face. I only had to get through breakfast and then I was out of there! Breakfast was delicious and we made small talk regarding venues and décor ideas for the wedding. We packed up the car, said our goodbyes, and headed for Athens. While the time spent in Tyrnavos was uncomfortable, I thought I could handle two days of this every year. Two days were fine.

Fast-forward one more year, and I didn't even want to spend thirty minutes alone with Fotini. We had decided to get married in Greece, which meant half of my family and a big chunk of my friends were paying a substantial amount to travel to Greece. Did they complain? Nope. They gladly paid their way to Greece and added to the amazing celebration of love we had during our wedding.

Fotini, on the other hand, brought all the negativity. She constantly made comments that we shouldn't get married on the Greek island we chose. In her mind, we should have gotten married close to where she lived. She called my wedding planners, without asking me or Vasilis, to ask them for the details of our wedding. Our wedding planners told Fotini in a respectful way that they could only discuss the wedding with the people who signed the contract. Best wedding planners ever! But that didn't stop Fotini from interfering.

The day before the wedding, at the beach pre-party we planned, she was again only negative. She didn't say much to me all day and ended the day by telling me we must give out the wedding favors outside the church according to tradition. When I tried to explain we would have the wedding favors at the last venue of the evening so guests wouldn't need to carry them around, she was not happy. Instead of getting into a fight, I just asked Vasilis to talk to her. I left and went to my hotel to eat and sleep before the big day.

The wedding was one of the best days of my life—we were surrounded with so much love, got married on a beautiful island, and ate and danced until the wee hours of the morning. I couldn't have asked for a better day. I could have asked for a better mother-in-law, though. She complained throughout the whole process, yelled at our photographer, and then told our wedding planners they did a horrible job because the wedding didn't follow some Greek traditions. Vasilis and I were aware of some of these traditions but opted to bypass them so there would be more time for mingling, eating, drinking and dancing. No one else complained. Fotini didn't dance at all during the wedding because we didn't play songs from her part of Greece. This was a joint decision we made because the music was way too slow and we wanted to keep the party lively. We played plenty of Greek music to which everyone, Greeks and non-Greeks alike, danced. You would think that seeing her son happy, in love, and everyone enjoying themselves would have made her happy. Nope! Instead she left the following morning very early with her daughter and son-in-law. She took the wedding gift back and said if Vasilis wanted the gift he would have to go to Tyrnavos and spend time with her. That was it. Not a single thank you to my family, who traveled around the world or contributed to the wedding.

What was her answer for her behavior? The wedding was too American. So I guess having a wedding in Greece, in a Greek-Orthodox church where the priest spoke only Greek, and having Greek food served and a Greek wedding singer was too American for her? Of course, there were some American traditions—I am half American after all. But to say that was an American wedding was way out of line. I still bit my tongue and after the honeymoon, Vasilis went to spend time with his mother and family. I opted to go spend time with my grandparents since I only had two more weeks, and time with them was precious. Did Vasilis' mother ever give a gift? Nope. Did she care that we paid extra for her family members who RSVP'd and then never showed up? Nope. Did she ever apologize to me? Nope.

In the end I got blamed because I chose to not go to Tyrnavos with Vasilis but spent time with my grandparents. I didn't care, and I am glad I made the choice I did. I needed time to cool off, but I definitely did not have plans to shut Vasilis' mother out of my life. Five months later, though, I was ready.

December 15, 2016 was a horrible day. I received a call from Greece that my beloved grandmother, who I was named after, passed away. After seventy-one years of being together, my ninety-year-old grandfather had to say goodbye to the love of his life. I was sick to my stomach and in shock. This couldn't be. My grandmother, Mary Fallaris, was so much of my identity and was a role model for the mother, wife, and matriarch I wanted to be. Books could be written about this amazing woman, and all my family, friends, and even colleagues knew how much my grandmother Mary meant to me.

Did I ever get a call from Fotini, my mother-in-law, saying she was sorry for my loss? No. Instead, three days after my grandmother's passing, she called my grandfather's apartment. My father answered the phone. My father tried to explain they were busy as my grandfather was loudly weeping in the background. It wasn't a good time. My entire family's only concern was keeping my grandfather supported, loved, and healthy during this grieving time. Did Fotini care? No. She quickly expressed her condolences and then asked why Vasilis and I had not called her. Out of respect for my grandfather and to avoid causing more distress, my father stayed calm but reiterated the hard time they were going through and kindly requested any questions be directed to Vasilis. He ended the conversation. He promptly told Vasilis and me the story, and I immediately told Vasilis to tell Fotini to never call my family again. Rage filled me and she was lucky I was thousands of miles away. How dare she call to ask about selfish interests when my family just suffered a huge loss.

That was it, I was done. I told Vasilis I was done. He understood and didn't fight me. To disrespect me and our wedding was one thing. To disrespect my grandmother and my grieving family crossed an unforgivable line. The whole year I did not call Fotini and she did not call me. I didn't care. She spread rumors about me in her town to her friends, telling anyone who would listen what a bad daughter-in-law I was. I didn't care. I didn't fight back.

Summer 2017 came and since I had started a new job, I only had nine days to go to Greece. It was important since it was the first summer without my grandmother and I wanted to be there to bring some cheer to my grandfather. My grandparents had built a summer home on the Greek island of Evia, and I had been summering on that island since I was born. Memories of our family parties, life friendships made, and love always come to mind when I think of Agiokambos, the village where our summer home was located. August 15 is the name day for anyone named Maria, Panagiota, Panagiotis, and any other rendition of the name of the Virgin Mary. It was a big day, as both my grandma Mary and I shared that name day, and she always had a big party with food and dancing. This would be the first name day without her and that was big. So I made sure to be with my family on that special day.

Did I mention my mother-in-law's middle name was Panagiota? That meant it was her name day too. I had not called her to tell her I was in Greece. I felt no need to after how she had behaved. I did write my brother-in-law, whom I adored and who stood up for me, that while I wished I could go see him, I could not, as I only had nine days, and after the loss our family suffered, I needed to be there for my grandfather and father. He completely understood. Fotini did not. The day before my name day my father got a call from Fotini during lunchtime. I asked him not to answer and he complied. Later that night, at around 10 p.m., she called the main line, which did not have caller identification. I answered and she announced herself. My chest hurt.

"I heard you were in town," she stated. I explained that it was only for nine days and given our family loss, I needed to be close to them. She proceeded to tell me they only saw me for thirty minutes after the wedding and that is all she saw of the new bride. I reiterated that the loss of my grandma was very hard on the family and I needed to be with my grandfather. I did wish Fotini an early happy name day. She

56

thanked me, and I don't know if she offered me well wishes for my name day. I can't remember because I was filled with rage since the woman still had not acknowledged the death of my grandmother or sent her condolences. I told her I had to go and politely found a way to hang up. I was supposed to get ready to go out to a club with friends but instead I started feeling sick— my chest hurt, my head hurt, and I felt a cold coming on. I could not be sick for my name day, as I needed to be an emotional support to my family and bring some cheer. I canceled my plans and went to bed. I don't believe in the evil eye usually, but in this case I strongly believe Fotini's negative energy transferred through the phone and my anger exacerbated my feeling ill.

The good news is I woke up feeling 100 percent better and celebrated with my family in my grandmother's honor. The bad news is I didn't talk to Fotini until I had to in December 2017. I was past three months pregnant, and she called Vasilis to wish him a happy birthday. She wanted to talk to me, so I listened. I wished her a happy birthday for her son and she asked how I was feeling. I said fine. She then said that we should call her more often. I quickly replied she had our number and could call us as well. Then I said I had to go and gave the phone to Vasilis. I wasn't going to subject my unborn child to negativity.

I work on my anger daily, but some days it gets the best of me. However, my continual work on my anger has allowed me to calm down and put things into perspective, as my intent is not to shut Fotini out of my life. I try to focus on the good, and there is a lot. I mean, she did raise the incredible man I married. Fotini has tried a couple times to call, and I do my best to be cordial. I start with cordial and work my way to familial. I will always keep positive hope that we can mend things as I know family is most important. That means I have to let go of anger and promise to give Fotini a fresh start.

When Vasilis calls her, I do make an effort to pass my well wishes along and be kind. I have pledged that I will not keep my son or Vasilis from Fotini or from his side of the family. That would mean I would become the womenemy. The sad truth, though, is Vasilis has seen less of his mother, and it was all his choice. Fotini blames me, but I guess as my friend puts it, it is better to blame me than face the reality that her own son needs breaks from her from time to time.

The lesson here to all mothers is to be kind to your daughter-in-law. Disagreements will happen, and that is fine. But be respectful and try to understand how negative actions have consequences including hurting another woman who will one day carry your grandchildren. Be careful, because if you push it too far, you will only hurt your son and cause him to separate himself from you.

I will remain hopeful that my mother-in-law will see her mistakes and fix them, just like my grandmother did. Read on to see how a stubborn Greek woman can change her ways and embrace a foreign daughter-in-law.

<u>Lesson:</u> Embrace Your Daughter-In-Law, And If You Don't At First, Fix Your Mistakes

My yiayia, which means *grandmother* in Greek, was a tough mother-in-law. She was tough on her first-born son's wife, and she was Greek! Then along came my mother—an

American who got pregnant (with me) out of wedlock. Being American was already a strike against her. In Greek there is a saying: it is better to go with the old and used shoe from your homeland than a foreign new shoe. Lovely saying, isn't it? Plus, Greek mothers thought all American women, especially the ones like my mother who backpacked unsupervised around Europe, were sluts, or as my yiayia liked to say, *butanes*. And then my mom went and got pregnant without being married. Did my yiayia put any blame on her son? Nope. It was all the American's fault. But that didn't stop my yiayia from swiftly planning the wedding of my father and mother within a month.

My mom, at five months pregnant, wasn't showing in her wedding dress and obliged to having a Greek Orthodox wedding, in Greece, with only Greek traditions. The only thing she wanted to do after the ceremony was change into a more comfortable dress for the reception. Did my yiayia allow this? Nope. The new dress would show the baby bump, and my yiayia did not want any of her friends knowing my mother was pregnant. Funny, though, that my yiayia never thought about what people would say when I was born four months later. Sometimes logic doesn't win.

My mother stayed in Greece with my dad for my first nine months of life. For my first summer on Earth, she took me to Agiokambos to be with my Greek family. My yiayia would cook daily meals for everyone and my mother enjoyed the delicious cooking. My mother, being a smart cookie, did not try to compete in the kitchen with my yiayia but rather thanked my yiayia on a daily basis for all the food and let my yiayia rule the kitchen. My grandparents felt love toward my mother automatically, as she gave them another grandchild (and might I say, a very cute one at that). My mother recognized my yiayia was queen of the kitchen and avoided even trying to cook for the family. This made my yiayia even more loving toward my mother. Things continued smoothly on after that until my parents moved to the United States.

Months after arriving in the US, my parents decided to divorce. My parents, while great friends, realized they were not meant to be a couple, and staying in a loveless marriage for the sake of a child would be detrimental to all. In the US, divorce is as common as getting braces. Greeks take marriage very seriously. So you would think that my mother would then have three strikes against her—American, pregnant out of wedlock, and divorcing my grandparents' youngest son. However, my yiayia, and therefore my papou (grandpa), because the woman runs the house in Greece, gave my mother a reprieve.

My yiayia saw that even when she was harsh with my mother, my mother didn't avoid her and never kept me, the granddaughter, from my yiayia. Furthermore, my mother granted my father's wish to name me after my yiayia. That is a heart melter right there. Even after the divorce, my mother wrote letters to my yiayia, sacrificed seeing me for three months every summer to send me to Greece, and always enforced how important it was to be close to my father and my Greek culture. My yiayia beyond appreciated this and showed her appreciation by visiting my mother every time she was in the US, writing letters back to my mother, and thanking my mother for raising me in the manner in which she did.

The last year of my yiayia's life included my wedding in Greece. My yiayia requested that she and my papou be seated at my mother's table next to my mother and stepdad. During the wedding, with tears coming down her cheeks, my yiayia thanked my mother again for all she did to raise me and to send me to Greece to bond with the Greek family. It meant the world to my yiayia. And it didn't stop there. After the wedding, my yiayia insisted my mother and stepdad stay in the summer home with my grandparents, my father, and the whole family. There was no tension and they also embraced my stepdad, whom they knew for decades. Now THAT is love.

My yiayia, proud as she was, might never have apologized to my mother for calling her an *American butana*, but through her actions she showed her love and appreciation. As I wrote the first draft of this chapter, I was seven months pregnant with my first child, a son, and as I previously mentioned, I already felt the instinctual *no one is good enough for my boy*. I set a goal for myself to fight that urge and remind myself to be embracing and loving toward my son's love interest, as I knew how it felt to be treated terribly by my mother-in-law. I also pledged that if I did make the mistake and prejudged, I would be woman enough, like my yiayia, to reverse my actions through love and acceptance. And maybe even take it one step further and apologize if I make such mistakes.

Chapter 7

Don't Be That Bridesmaid

This will be the shortest chapter. I have heard numerous stories of friendships being ruined because someone was a horrible bridesmaid. The stress of the wedding kicks in, jealousy comes out, and people forget the purpose of the wedding is to celebrate the love of two human beings. I have seen bridesmaids ignore the bride; make her cry during the bachelorette trip; flirt with a married groomsman in front of the wife during the wedding; change out of the bridesmaid dress before pictures because the dress was too uncomfortable; cry loudly during the entire ceremony, distracting guests; and make a commotion during the speech part of the wedding. This just screams "I don't give a crap about your day...or your happiness" and is unacceptable.

I was blessed with eleven bridesmaids who supported me, cheered for me, de-stressed me when I was anxious, and truly showed they were happy about my happiness. They even flew to a Greek island to show their devotion.

Going into details of stories I have witnessed and heard would be just for the purpose of providing juicy, negative details, which is not productive since the lesson is very straightforward.

<u>Lesson:</u> If You Accept The Role Of Bridesmaid, Be Happy And Support The Bride

If you don't want to be a bridesmaid, are jealous of the bride, or mad you were not picked as maid of honor, just decline being a bridesmaid. If you have already accepted being a bridesmaid and feel one of these feelings, just suck it up and be happy, or act happy, for the woman who has given you the honor to stand by her as she embarks on this new journey in her life.

Chapter 8

Don't Be A Mother-Judger

Have you ever realized the word "mother-fudger" (hint: I am using the PG version here) is a bad word and it includes the word *mother*? Think about it. Most of the time that word is used to insult another, and the word *mother* has to be used as part of it. Or the phrase "save the drama for your mama"? Where is papa? Why do we only give mama drama? Why is the word *mother* linked to insults or judgment?

It seems women are judged about being mothers prior to them even getting pregnant. Sayings like "you should get that out of your system as you can't be as free when you are a mother" or "enjoy your easy life of sleeping in now that you don't have children and a husband."

Those comments are inherently judgmental. Who says a woman's life without a child (and husband, at that) is easy? Are you living her life? Who says the woman will even want children? I was nine months pregnant when I started writing this chapter, and I wanted to explore the scenarios I experienced or witnessed that bring about or induce (yes, I had labor terms on my brain) judgment.

What I learned from my experiences and my explorations: uplift, support, and help the woman to be the best version of herself without judgment. No one can know what is best for her except HER.

To Have Children vs. Not To Have Children

"What is wrong with her to not want children? No wonder she is such a witch. That is unnatural." To the majority of this world, a woman is deemed abnormal if she doesn't want kids. Yes, our bodies are made to produce children, but with that same argument, men's bodies are made to impregnate woman until the day they die. But you don't see many men in their seventies wanting to procreate, do you? And do we judge them? Nope!

I have friends who choose not to have children. They love children and spoil their friends and family who have children, but for them, they have made that choice to live without the experience of having children. Good for them! That is a smart choice. What would be stupid is to have children just because the world tells you to. That would not be fair to the child or the parents.

Being An "Old" Pregnant Woman

At thirty-five years old, I was technically having a Geriatric Pregnancy. Can you believe that? Me? Geriatric! Get the hell out of here. It is true that women's bodies are prime for baby making in their early twenties. That doesn't mean the psychological or emotional state of the woman is ready. If they are, that is great. But if they want to go to school, receive a graduate degree, work and establish themselves first before having a child, that is okay too!

Many people think that women getting pregnant in their late thirties and early forties is not smart. Yes, there are higher risks of passing on genetic diseases, but we have this thing called technology that can screen for everything and give the mother choices. Also, people are being judgmental when they say that in their late thirties and early forties, these women won't have the energy to take care of children. I call BS on that! My aunt is in her fifties with two teenagers and has more energy than me!

To sum up, as long as mother and child are healthy, a woman can have a baby WHENEVER she wants!

Weight Gain During Pregnancy

The moment I told my family I was pregnant, I had numerous people tell me to watch my weight, as my Greek side of the family tended to gain a lot of weight during pregnancy. Instead of focusing on this new amazing life inside of me, the worry of blowing up like a blimp consumed me. It didn't help that while I didn't show it, I had gained more in my first trimester than "average", and when my doctor said that, I started to break down. Even when my doctor said it was nothing to worry about since I was exercising and hadn't gain fat anywhere but my belly, I just pictured myself as a cow. I was seeing a personal trainer and eating healthy. I had always been a "heavier" girl on the scale even when I was smaller in size than women who weighed a lot less than me. I had been battling the heavy bone and muscle density traits I inherited and finally got over it as a pre-pregnant woman.

Okay, I digressed. It turned out I was in the minority in that I didn't gain a lot in my second and third trimester and it all went to belly and boobs. I was praised for looking beautiful and carrying a large belly. I finally felt happy. My doctor was happy, as I was exercising daily, and she told me I looked beautiful. So why did I have to deal with the fear of weight gain in pregnancy rather than just enjoying my pregnancy? Why did I let my judgmental Greek family member, who saw one photo of me and proclaimed I had gained too much weight, bother me? It was stupid.

This is not to say women should be unhealthy. I am not an advocate for that. But every woman is different. Some woman gain little weight and get judged for not eating more and others just naturally gain more and get judged that they are being lazy.

I say it really isn't anyone's business to comment and advise on weight unless they are a medical professional. Talking to a woman about her weight in pregnancy and reminding her to be careful just raises the stress level in the woman, which actually might cause weight gain. So let her be herself and let her know what a beautiful person she is for growing the miracle of life.

Weight Loss After Pregnancy

Unless you are a doctor or trainer, SHUT UP! A woman has just gone through one of the hardest physical tests anyone will go through and her hormones are in flux. Her body will take some time to get back to normal and the mother will be focusing on her new bundle of joy and learning how to be a mother. Do you think the stress of losing weight and the fear of "don't let yourself go" helps a mother? Nope! It just adds to her cortisol increase, which as mentioned above, can actually halt weight loss.

Comparison really needs to be avoided when it comes to weight loss. I have been present when these ladies told a new mom how their friend Jane lost all her baby weight four months after giving birth. While some people might provide these stories as inspiration that a mother can lose the weight quickly, what normally happens is the mom feels pressured to live up to how Jane lost the weight. It's great for Jane that she lost it all in four months. But another mom might take a year, and that is okay too. It depends on numerous factors, medically and financially. There are some who are fortunate to have a night nurse, lots of help, and physical trainers to help them kick-start the weight loss. There are others who can't afford the help, don't have family close by, and choose to sleep over working out, as they are in survival mode. And sometimes it just comes down to genetics and the way a woman's body works. Social media is the worst with "snap back body" photos. The end result is that the new mom stresses out over the comparisons, and aside from the negative consequences of stress, she loses the focus that she is doing an amazing job being a mother.

Epidural vs. Natural Birth

I struggled with this. Initially I was 100 percent sold with an epidural since all my friends did it and they told me it is the way to go as it makes the process more enjoyable. I totally get that. But as I read and took birth classes, I realized there are some benefits to natural birth—the adrenaline rush after giving birth, having complete feeling in your body, and being able to move around a lot more.

So I decided it would be a game time decision. I would opt for a natural birth, but if I couldn't handle the pain or didn't want to, I could always go for the epidural (assuming there was still time for it). That way, I wouldn't feel guilty if I didn't go through with the natural birth. But why should I feel "guilty"? Nothing is wrong with either way, but somehow I was coded to feel I was less of a woman if I went the "easy" route and got an epidural.

I am coded that way because there are those people, Greek women in particular, who say, "Go through a natural birth because the pain will bond you closer to your baby." Um, I think being in my belly for nine months is bonding enough, thank you very much.

And to address the "easy" route comment about an epidural—is the peanut gallery forgetting the contractions prior to the epidural? The tearing the woman will have to recover from after the birth, and all the fun other side effects of giving birth?

On the flip side, calling a woman crazy for having a natural birth isn't cool either. Maybe for them it is a personal goal to go through the journey naturally, just like their grandmother did.

So the lesson here? Support the mother's choice and give them room, judgment-free, to change their mind.

Side note: If you are wondering if I got the epidural, I did.

Ten hours into my twenty-six hours of labor, I couldn't take the contractions and asked for it. At first I felt guilty, like I was taking the easy way out. My friend and godmother to my son quickly pointed out there is no easy way out in giving birth and there is nothing to be ashamed of—I needed to do what was best for me and F what others thought. Well, God bless the epidural! My contractions were calmed and I was able to relax and regain strength. The kicker? The epidural didn't really work when it came time for the actual birth, so I felt everything. Yup, all 9.1 pounds and 22 inches of my son!

I stand by my lesson: give the mother whatever the F she needs to get that baby out of her belly!

Maternity Leave

As soon as I announced I was pregnant in the workplace, I frequently was asked, "How much time will you take off?" I just wanted to process there was a little boy, meaning a little penis, growing inside me! I received advice to take three to four weeks prior to my due date, and when I said I was working up until four days prior, I was called crazy. My explanation was that I would rather use the time off once my son was born to bond with him. But really, I owed no one an explanation.

Some women will want to take four months off, some will want to take three, and others will want to take a month. It is up to the mother and her partner on what they want to do. So again, please zip the lip!

Stay-At-Home Moms vs. Working Moms

I learned in a recent seminar on the elimination of bias in the workforce that even asking a woman if she plans to return to work is implicit bias in itself. That question is never asked of men, but people feel free to ask that of women.

There are mothers who judge other mothers for staying home, saying "a real job" makes them feel more independent. Do these women think that these stay-at-home moms are eating bonbons and watching TV all day? While not monetized, a mother's job is more than a full time job – it is a constant job with no vacation and no overtime pay - and calling it anything less than a "real job" is insulting. More than changing poopy diapers, feedings, and sleepless nights, a parent molds another human being and gives and maintains that child's life. That is as real as it gets!

Then there are moms who judge the women who go back to work. "Don't you love your child more than your career? How can you let someone else raise your child?" Okay, ladies, can we put the guns away? Those are very insulting questions. Some mothers have to work, as babies are expensive! Some mothers feel they are better mothers when they spend part of their day doing what they are passionate about and then come home refreshed to be a mother. They can do both. Some women feel they are better with having an identity outside the home, and that is fine too!

Breastfeeding vs. Bottle Feeding

Breast is best. We have all heard that, and many hospitals use that chant to promote breastfeeding. Yes, there are many health benefits for the baby and mama that result from breastfeeding. So if a mother is able to breastfeed and wants to, then go for it! I would like to add that there is not a requisite amount of time a woman should breastfeed. So please stop judging the mothers who breastfeed for a month or are still breastfeeding after eighteen months. Not your choice. As long as baby and mother are healthy, happy, and progressing, then that is what matters.

The danger of the push for breastfeeding is there are mothers who can't breastfeed or don't want to for many reasons which are personal. Some physically cannot, for some it is too painful, and some want to work and not be interrupted by pumping or breaking to feed. Yes, there are employment laws that give mothers breaks to pump. That does not mean the mother has to take breaks to pump. She might choose to have uninterrupted days or the idea of pumping disgusts her or it simply hurts. Or how about she just doesn't want to? Why does she have to explain herself to others?

Currently, the mother who does not breastfeed has instant societal pressures to explain why she is bottle-feeding. I know women who were judged by their own family members for not breastfeeding. One woman, Daphne, had a really hard time when her child was not latching. Her friends and mother-in-law called her daily, sometimes hourly, to ask Daphne if the child managed to latch or if he had another bottle. You can imagine the stress and sadness this caused Daphne. Daphne felt as if she wasn't a good enough mother. This is insane, as Daphne was an incredible mom and was trying to do everything in her power to be the best mom for her son. That is all you could ask, and should ask, from a mother.

But the insane pressure to breastfeed is there. I remember it took my son two weeks to really latch and my milk was delayed in coming in completely. He was supposed to have gained back the weight he lost from the hospital within the first two weeks, but that didn't happen. The pediatrician told me that until my baby could latch and my milk completely came in, I would need to supplement with formula. I was devastated and crying the whole car ride home. My husband tried to comfort me, but I was inconsolable. I felt horrible—like I wasn't providing for my son. The person who got through to me was my father. He asked why did I care how my son was getting fed. "What matters is he is getting fed. Who cares what others think? You are doing the best you can, and that is all that matters."

My dad was repeating the knowledge some medical professionals use—Fed Is Best. That is the correct way to view it. As long as baby is fed and healthy, and mom is healthy and happy, that is the best for all.

Unsolicited Advice To Moms

People who have birthed human beings think they have an unfettered right to provide advice to any new mom, whether the newbie mom wants such advice or not. Comments like "you should be sleeping more" and "you need to learn to put yourself first" and "don't worry about laundry and cleaning" can definitely come from a good place, but the result is not positive. The comment about sleeping more is just ridiculous. It makes the mom feel like she is doing something wrong because she doesn't have time to sleep. And then the mom stresses out that she isn't getting enough sleep, causing stress to overwhelm the mom and possibly cause her to lose even the little sleep she gets.

The word *should* triggers the mom to think she isn't doing the best she can. Also, when someone tells the mother to not worry about cleaning or laundry, it has the opposite effect. The mother now thinks about cleaning and laundry and therefore, in addition to navigating being a mother, she has these lingering thoughts of household chores. As I said, not the intent of the advice giver but a stressful result to the mama.

I have been that womenemy giving unsolicited advice. I have been blessed with a son who hasn't had a lot of problems with sleeping or eating. Two of my dear friends have children the same age as my son, and they would talk to me about how exhausted they were and couldn't seem to get their child to sleep more than four hours at a time, or their child needed to fall asleep in their arms. I would constantly tell them to put their baby in the crib while baby was awake and let the baby cry a little, as it would pass and the baby would learn to sleep on his own. That is what worked for my son, who cried for maybe five minutes the first three times we put him in his crib, and then he just entertained himself and went to sleep. So I thought all babies did that. Giving my friends this unsolicited advice just made them feel worse about their situation—like they were doing something wrong.

And actually, my friends were not doing anything wrong. I just got lucky. There are babies that are very particular with how they sleep, and for the mama to have any shot at sleeping, they do whatever it takes. Survival mode at its best. Recently our son kept us up for two nights, waking us up every two hours due to a cold. By the second night I told my husband I couldn't take it much longer. If anyone tried to tell me to let him cry it out or just block out the crying, I would want to dropkick them. And that was only after two nights! My friends have been dealing with it for eighteen months. I am surprised they didn't dropkick me—physically or verbally. The moral is not to give unsolicited advice, as it appears to be judgmental.

Lesson: Support The Mom In Whatever Allows Her To Be The Best Version Of Herself

Being an uplifter is key. My boss did a great job of that. I remember her calling just to see how I was doing being a new mom. When I explained my daily activities, she stopped me and said, "You deserve an award for even being able to brush your teeth!" That instantly made me feel better and laugh. It was so true. I was dealing with trying to feed my son every two or three hours, learn how to be a mother, take care of my postpartum body, and trying to function in general. I was constantly hard on myself, always pointing out all the things I didn't accomplish in the day. For my boss to flip it around and celebrate an accomplishment –hey, showering and brushing teeth are big accomplishments to a new mother—made me giggle and feel good about myself for accomplishing something. It was a definite boost because I felt someone understood how I felt and not only emphasized with me, but supported and uplifted me.

Allowing the woman to be the best version of herself

75

includes listening without providing advice, unless, of course, the woman asks. My friends Constandina, Jasmine, and Titika are the epitome of being great listeners with no judgment. I have talked to them about my fears of losing part of myself when I become a mom, the frustration of not having time for anything, and just feeling overwhelmed. Did they tell me to just sleep more and let someone else watch my child? Did they say I was silly to stress over things? Nope! They just let me vent and voiced their understanding. They would reiterate that what I was feeling was normal and give me examples of good things I was doing. Not just with motherhood, but with any struggle in my life, it is always easy to go to these friends as they truly are a safe place to talk.

Chapter 9

Don't Hook Up With Your Friend's Ex

This is a no-no. This is not the whole "I planted my flag there first" thing as guys tend to think. Women take it more personally and emotionally. When they decide to be involved in a relationship, they are attached emotionally and feel it is a private relationship. For a friend to start a different private relationship with the same person feels like an emotional intrusion and betrayal. Usually, it is not a betrayal because the woman has not moved on, but more of a discomfort with a friend pursuing a very deep relationship with a person she might never want to see again. Questions like, "Why would she want to be with someone who treated me so poorly?" arise. Sometimes the woman will wonder if their friend was after their boyfriend even before he became an ex. This adds a level of betrayal and suspicion of the sincerity of the friendship.

Not to mention, it is awkward, as friends are supposed to be forever, but exes usually can be removed from your life. So a friend dating an ex means the ex never leaves the picture.

Now, there is an exception to this "don't hook up with a friend's ex" rule—if you ask for permission and discuss it with the friend first.

I didn't get this rule when I was younger. I had just broken up with my fiancé and I was a mess. I went to a party and the ex of one of my best friends, Dina, was there. Dina and her ex were on very good terms, and it had been years since they dated. Dina was in a serious relationship and was very happy. When I went to this party, which was in a hotel, I found myself talking to the ex, Anthony. We had known each other for years, as our circle of friends were intertwined.

The news of my broken engagement and the fact that after ten years I was newly single had spread like wildfire. At the party we all drank, laughed, danced, and drank some more. I was spending the night in another friend's room but ended up talking for hours to Anthony and his friends. Anthony was getting cuddly with me, and after being cheated on and breaking off my soon-to-be nuptials, I liked the attention. However, as the night came to a close, my moral compass guided me to say I should be heading to my friend Kiki's room. While I liked the attention and I knew Dina was completely over (I mean SO over) Anthony, something didn't feel right.

Anthony begged me to stay—just to talk and cuddle. At that point Kiki walked in, and I said I was going with her. She stopped me and told me to stay in Anthony's room for the night. I looked at her, and she gave me the "it's okay, Dina won't care" look. While deep down I still knew it wasn't right, the alcohol in my system combined with my yearning for male attention won, and I stayed the night. I never kissed or did anything further with Anthony besides cuddling. Scout's honor.

In the morning I did the walk of shame home—is it still a walk of shame if no sexual conduct happened? Moving on. I called Dina that day and told her everything, which wasn't much, but I wanted to get off my chest that I had cuddled with her ex. She giggled it off, but I could tell it was a nervous laugh. Then for the next week, I got radio silence. I knew something was up. I finally texted her and she admitted that she was upset, not because she wanted Anthony back or that she wasn't happy with her current relationship, but she and I were best friends and it felt like a betrayal. While at the time I didn't get it because I loved her 100 percent and would never do anything to hurt her, I still apologized because in her eyes, I had betrayed her and I needed to apologize for that.

I would later find out how it felt to be in Dina's shoes.

Years later, I was married and over my ex-fiancé as well as two other guys I dated prior to meeting my husband. I had a close friendship with one of those exes, Sebastion. Sebastion was a skilled artist who could paint and play music. While our relationship didn't work out, I was blessed to call him a friend, and I introduced him to my close circle of friends. I especially made a point to introduce him to Betty, an up-and-coming writer. She was looking for fresh artwork for her book cover, and I suggested she take a look at Sebastion' work.

Betty called me to tell me she loved Sebastion' work, and he had agreed to paint the book cover for her. I was ecstatic, as I enjoyed helping my friends professionally. I did notice Betty would bring up Sebastion' name a lot, and one night she called me to tell me she had taken Sebastion out for drinks to thank him for painting her book cover. I got this weird feeling that she wasn't telling me the whole story, and I thought it was weird that she hadn't invited me to go out with them. She explained that she thought I was tired, but I thought to myself—that had not stopped her before. Betty went on how at drinks, her other friends were present and told her she should date Sebastion since he was single, tall, and extremely handsome. I told Betty he was a great guy, and I asked her if she was interested. "No, of course not," she said. Though I felt strongly she was interested, I just left it at that as she might not have been ready to share that with me yet.

Months later, out of the blue, I got a message from Betty saying she needed to talk to me, as there was something she needed to tell me and she felt very guilty about it. Betty and I talked daily, so I knew it was serious since she could have just brought it up in our frequent conversations. I instantly had a gut feeling it had to do with Sebastion.

The next day, Betty called me and let me know that a month prior, she kissed Sebastion. Sharp pains vibrated through my chest, but I just listened. She said she didn't want it to happen, but she was out and he was flirting with her and they kissed. She apologized over and over again. "Why didn't you just tell me you liked him? I could tell you did," were the words that came out of my mouth. Betty claimed she didn't think she liked him, but to outside people it was clear she did. She said it took time for her to realize what everyone, including me, saw. I felt she was lying and playing the "dumb" card to make the whole situation easier on me. That was not the truth of what happened (she really didn't know if she liked him), but it was how I felt in my state of shock/anger/reflection. I could tell she was frightened to lose me, and I knew she was a genuinely good person who wouldn't want to hurt me. I chose to focus on that last thought.

I took a deep breath and composed myself, as I had to be very careful how I explained my hurt. I explained to Betty that my hurt was not because I wasn't happily married or that I wanted to be with Sebastion. It was because she didn't come to me first, but rather it felt like she went behind my back. What Sebastion and I shared was very, very special to me. At a time when I was most unsure of myself after my ex-fiancé, and when I was still getting to know who I was as a woman, Sebastion made me feel beautiful, free, and adventurous. I gained my confidence back and I explored ways to express myself. For all of those gifts, I hold Sebastion in very high regard, and I am thankful I dated him. Betty knew all of this, and for her to not be honest with me felt like a betrayal and disregard of something special to me.

I explained that if Betty just had been honest with me, I would have given her the green light. Yes, it would have been weird, but both Betty and Sebastion are great people, and I only want them to be happy. As a friend, I would also feel honored that Betty came to me first, as it would show she acknowledged my feelings.

While Betty's action stung for a couple of days, I also knew she was genuinely sorry and her intent was not to betray me or hurt me. I knew she was probably scared to admit to me that she liked my ex, and that is why she kept it from me. I also thought that she could have just blocked herself from the thought of even liking him. As I thought some more, it dawned on me what I needed to be focusing on and remembering - I knew Betty to be a very kind, giving and loyal friend. Because of the amazing person Betty is, and because I knew how it felt to be in Betty's shoes, I forgave her and said she should date Sebastion if she wanted to. Both are still my close friends today.

Lesson: Avoid the Hook-Up; If You Want More Than A Hook-Up Ask Your Friend First

My advice to all women is if you just want to have a hookup with a man, avoid your friend's ex. It is not worth a short-lived night. However, if you have real feelings for a friend's ex, approach your friend, be honest about your feelings, and ask if it would be okay to date the ex. While it might be one of the hardest things you do, your friend will respect you and trust you more for your honesty and ethics.

Chapter 10

Don't Automatically Hate Your Significant Other's Platonic Female Friend

Okay, so far we have covered being welcoming to another woman at work and being welcoming to a future female member of the family (aka your daughter-in-law). There is another woman we need to be welcoming to—the platonic female friend of your significant other. There is a very common occurrence when a female meets their significant other's female friend—they are suspicious. The suspicion is twofold: (1) Does the female friend secretly want more from the friendship? (2) Does the significant other have secret feelings for the female friend? This suspicion creates an invisible barrier between two women who could otherwise be friends. Here is a challenge to us all—let's try embracing the female friend before passing judgment. Just like there is room for a woman in someone's workplace and in someone's family, there is no limit to the female friends we can make. Who knows—a deep friendship could be formed since both woman obviously are important to a common person in their lives (the significant other).

Growing up I was a tomboy—I played a ton of sports and had many guy friends. To this day, I have many male friends and I consider them as family. If any guy I dated had a problem with me being close with my guy friends, I would break up with him on the spot as my male friends are like brothers to me. I have been lucky for the most part that I have not run into that conflict with any of the guys I dated or the amazing husband I married. However, I do know how it feels to be the friend who is disliked by the girlfriend of my male friend.

In college, one of my best friends was Bobby. Since freshman year we told each other everything and he was my bodyguard, always protecting me. My college boyfriend and Bobby became very good friends as well, and we seemed like a big family. Junior year came and Bobby started dating Cathy. Cathy was different than the other ladies Bobby dated, as he seemed very serious about her. Cathy was pretty, smart, and ambitious. I was thrilled to meet her, and my wish of finally being able to go on double dates with Bobby were close to becoming a reality.

I was sensitive to the possibility that Cathy might be a little guarded because of the fact that Bobby and I were so close. Bobby would confide in me about everything, drop what he was doing to help me, and occasionally crash on my couch. To me, he was family, and there was nothing untoward happening. However, I could see how others, especially in the gossip mill that is college, would spread rumors that Bobby and I were more than friends. It didn't bother me, as I knew the truth, but I didn't want anything to get in the way of Cathy and Bobby's budding romance.

So I invited Cathy to have a girls' dinner at my apartment during the summer. We were both taking summer classes to get ahead for the next year. I really appreciated Cathy's nerdiness and the fact that we both wanted to go to law school. Cathy and I had a lovely evening and she enjoyed my cooking—I was relieved! We then talked over some cheap wine. I was so excited to have made a new friend, and even better, she was the girlfriend of one of my best friends. As I drove her back to her place, she brought up a recent complication Bobby had with his summer job. I concurred that his boss wasn't treating him correctly and mentioned I was shocked to hear about it the night before. Cathy got a bit quiet, but I just took it that she was mad about the situation as well. As I dropped Cathy off, she thanked me for the girls' night and said we should all get together soon. After a great night, I could sense the double date was around the corner.

Well, I totally misread that situation, since that double date never came. The first couple days I didn't hear a lot from Bobby, just shorter texts and such. I knew he was busy so I just assumed that was the cause. Then when my boyfriend came back from drinks with Bobby, I was confused as to why I wasn't invited but shrugged it off to a boys' night out. When I finally got Bobby on the phone, I wanted to tell him about the girls' night and how great I thought Cathy was. My gushing was cut short.

"Mari, why did you have to tell her I told you about my work complication?" I was totally confused. I mentioned that Cathy brought it up and I was just agreeing with her. Bobby explained it wasn't that I knew about the situation, it was that he told me *first*, the night before he told her. Apparently Cathy was upset that Bobby confided in me first, and she wasn't comfortable with our friendship. I wanted to call Cathy immediately to tell her there was nothing to be uncomfortable or worried about, but Bobby begged me to let it go. He said it would blow over. My best friend's wishes were my command, and I retreated.

One thing men don't understand is that women don't just let

things blow over if there is no resolution. In Cathy's mind, I was too close to her man, and that had not been resolved. At every event, Cathy was cordial and gave me the obligatory Puerto Rican one-kiss-on-the-cheek to greet me. But there was this invisible wall, which was chilly, between us. The more I tried to be sweet, the more I felt her pull back from trying to get to know me. I could feel her friends eye me when I walked over to talk to Bobby. I could tell that to Cathy's friends, I was the womenemy.

When I tried to tell my boyfriend how hurt I was, he just shrugged it off to women being women. Too much drama for him. Surprised I am not married to him? Okay, I digressed again.

I decided to give up trying to beg for Cathy's friendship or approval and just vowed I would be respectful to her and continue to be Bobby's best friend. Cathy's growing reluctance about me made it more difficult to see Bobby. We couldn't go on double dates, and while Bobby didn't admit it, I noticed he was not coming over to hang out as much. He did have time for hanging out with my boyfriend, and for the first time, I was jealous of the man I was dating. I mean, Bobby was my best friend first and if I had a penis, none of this drama would have mattered!

Then the beginning of the end happened. My boyfriend and I got in a massive fight, and I was so upset I drove over to Bobby's house in the middle of the night because I felt I was having an anxiety attack. Bobby calmed me down and let me stay over. He then left me to go talk to my boyfriend, as he knew my boyfriend was in the wrong. As I previously mentioned, Bobby was like my brother and would have my back no matter what. The collegial romantic tiff was resolved by morning, and I thanked Bobby for standing up for me. "Anytime, Mari," he responded.

My fight was over, but Bobby's fight had just begun, unbeknownst to him. When word on the "college street" got to Cathy that I had spent the night at Bobby's house, she was livid. She thought it was totally inappropriate that I spent the night. Side note: I spent the night on the couch and Bobby lived with two other guys and a woman. Nevertheless, Cathy just focused on her interpretation of the story: I fought with my boyfriend and ran to Bobby. In her mind, I was choosing Bobby over my boyfriend because I secretly wanted to be with him. Ahh, the inner workings of a woman's mind. The CIA, FBI, and Harvard neurological department (if that exists, it sounds fancy) are still trying to figure out a woman's mind.

While the theory that I wanted Bobby romantically could not be further from the truth, Cathy stuck to that theory without a scrap of evidence. Not the signs of a great lawyer in the making.

Bobby, not wanting to lose his relationship with Cathy, called me and said that he had to take a break from our friendship. He couldn't be the person between my boyfriend and me, and it was causing strife with Cathy. I called BS—I had been the "middlewoman" with Bobby's prior relationships or his friendships, and I always was there to help him. I knew he didn't mind being my confidant and protector when it came to my college boyfriend. I knew what was really happening—Cathy was using my relationship drama as an excuse to break up my friendship with Bobby. She didn't like that I was one of his best friends who he confided in, complimented, and cared for. Again, if I had a penis, my relationship drama would not have mattered.

As I cried on the phone about how Bobby was being unfair, Bobby promised we just couldn't be friends for a couple weeks so Cathy could see there was nothing between us. He promised he loved me like a sister and would always be there for me. He just needed a couple weeks to prove his love to Cathy. I didn't have any choice—I accepted it and then cried myself to sleep.

The next couple weeks came and went, and I was sad. I couldn't call Bobby to tell him a funny story or update him on my applications to law school. I was in my senior year and would be moving to the West Coast following graduation. I missed going back to his hometown in Boston to see his family, who were my surrogate family since mine was on the other end of the country. As my four years of collegiate experience were coming to an end in New England, I felt a big chunk of my experience, meaning my friendship with Bobby, was being erased.

My sadness turned to anger as the fall semester was coming to a close. One night my boyfriend was late coming home, and I called to ask him how much longer before he brought over my favorite pasta for dinner. He was at the restaurant and was going to get my order but admitted he was having a drink and hanging with Bobby. Oh, so my boyfriend could hang out with him, just not me? Nice. When my boyfriend came home, my blood sugar had dropped from hunger, so I quickly opened my pasta container to find the wrong pasta. "Oops, that means Bobby ate your pasta," my boyfriend said. Usually, I would laugh it off. But not this time. "_____ HIM," I said. (You fill in the expletive, hint—it is four letters). My boyfriend froze. I was pissed. I got dumped as a best friend, but my boyfriend got to inherit my best friend, and my best friend then eats my favorite pasta. _____ him and _____the whole situation. (Again, fill in the expletives). Who did I blame? Cathy! Of course, I also blamed Bobby, as he should have had the balls to stand up to Cathy, but Cathy was the one who instigated all this pain over an unfounded theory that something was going on or could be going on between Bobby and me.

Fueled by my anger, I vowed that if Bobby and I ever became friends again, I would not give a damn about Cathy's feelings. I wanted her out of his life! Not because I wanted Bobby as a boyfriend, but because she took my best friend from me for no reason. Yes, I realize I was being the vindictive womenemy and Bobby was also to blame, but my anger didn't allow me to think correctly.

When I saw Bobby in public, I would go give him a big hug in front of Cathy. Bobby, being the gentleman he was, was not going to refuse a hug from me, a woman who had his back through college. I made sure to be very dressed up every time we all went to a party and would purposefully go over to Cathy and say a fake "hello" just so she could see how amazing I looked. Since she and her stupid girl squad thought I was the womenemy, I stooped to their level and became one. And I didn't give a crap.

Bobby and I weren't friends like we used to be, but through my boyfriend I would find out Cathy was nagging Bobby and was extremely jealous of all women. Bobby was not happy with his relationship and didn't know what to do. Well, I didn't feel bad for him. Every time my boyfriend would talk about how he felt bad for Bobby and his situation, I would think *karma is a B*!

Then, finally, the breakup happened right at the beginning of spring semester. YIPEEEEEEEEEEEE! The witch was gone! As I have previously stated, I try not to be the woman to celebrate another woman's pain. But after all the strife Cathy caused me, I didn't care. Slowly Bobby started calling more and coming around. I finally confronted him and told him how he hurt me, and he deeply apologized and promised never to do that again. He opened up over everything Cathy had put him through and how he was relieved to be done with her. I listened and was empathetic, as breakups suck, regardless of whether the relationship was toxic.

At a spring party, Cathy and her girl squad showed up. I was talking to Bobby and my boyfriend. I could feel the squad's eyes on me and I could feel their anger rising. What did I do? I just turned and gave them a smile. Look who was left standing?

I definitely made a mistake—I used my anger toward Cathy's actions as an excuse to become a womenemy. I did things I was not proud of and I do apologize for that. The big lesson from this is to embrace the friends of your boyfriend, husband, and partner, whether they be female or male. If they are female, don't automatically assume something untoward is happening. Give the woman a chance. If the woman is shady, it will show. But if she is truly a good person, you might gain another friend.

<u>Lesson:</u> Embrace the Female Friend Of Your Significant Other

I have recently gained a dear friend, Gabriela, because she embraced me as the female friend to her husband. Her husband Jordan and I were incredibly close at the time she started dating him. Jordan would always refer to me as his sister.

Gabriela took her time to get to know me. She admits she always has her guard up more with new people but always gives them a chance. Well, she gave me a chance—a truly genuine chance to be her friend. I got to know her through group hangouts with her and Jordan. All seemed like it was going well, and I got to know her more and more. Jordan and Gabriela flew to Greece for my wedding, Jordan was a groomsman, and they both mingled and connected with my family and friends. Things were going in the right direction.

A couple months later Jordan and Gabriela were engaged. I was thrilled for Jordan as Gabriela was his dream woman. I couldn't shake the worry I had based on my experience with Cathy, that maybe I would lose my closeness with Jordan. But I tried to keep my fears at bay.

I received a call from Gabriela a couple months prior to their wedding. She wanted to meet me for a workout and dinner. A very Orange County way to hang out. I enjoyed the dinner, and even the workout, but mostly I enjoyed getting to know her more. Then she said she had something to talk to me about. I got a knot in my stomach—*was I calling Jordan too much?* I was worried I had done something to upset Gabriela, and all the Cathy memories started to flood my brain. Before my crazy mind got too ahead of itself, Gabriela stated that one of her bridesmaids could not be in the wedding anymore, and since I was like a sister to Jordan and Gabriela wanted to become closer to me, she wanted to ask me to be a bridesmaid. I screamed YES and started to tear up. Just the sentiment of asking me meant the world to me.

The wedding was an amazing experience, and it allowed me to get to truly know the amazing person Jordan was marrying. Gabriela and I talk frequently, sometimes more than I talk with

Jordan, and she was such a support to me during my pregnancy. I am forever grateful to Gabriela for getting to know me and not judging me as a female friend to her man. Now I have my brother and a new dear friend.

Chapter 11

Don't Be A Womenemy To Yourself

Womenemies mean we are enemies to each other as women, and that includes being enemies to ourselves. We are definitely our worst enemies at times. For example:

1. We have imposter syndrome—when we get a promotion or are in a certain successful part of our life, we think it is due to luck, and others will eventually find out that we are a scam and we aren't qualified to have the success we have.

2. When we get a compliment, instead of saying just "thank you", we feel we need to credit our success to others or say it was luck or say "thank you, but I could have done a bit better".

3. We constantly "should ourselves"—I should be skinnier, I should be less stressed, I should cook more, I should spend more time with my kids, I should spend more time at work, I should be at a different stage in my life, I should be married with kids by now. And the list goes on and on and on, and on and on and on.

4. We compare ourselves to the others we see on social media.

5. When we make a mistake, we beat ourselves up.

6. We don't ask or are uncomfortable to ask for a raise or to be compensated fairly.

7. We wait until we have every qualification for a job before applying for our dream job, even if that takes years. Side note: men just apply, even if they don't have every qualification.

8. We put others' needs in front of our own needs.

I have been in violation of all of these. The year 2019 was one of the hardest of my life. Great news happened—I got a new job as a VP of an amazing and fast-growing law firm, and we moved to Marina Del Rey, a dream I always had. My father from Greece pledged to come out for six months to watch our son as we tried to save and prepare for the investment that is LA childcare. Well, upon my dad arriving, he soon had severe health complications that demanded I add caretaker to the long list of duties I already had (wife, mom, VP, daughter, friend). We had to find childcare, navigate the emergency room system of LA USC, and I had to deal with balancing a full-time job with motherly/wifely duties. Months later my father was stable; we had childcare and my father wanted to return to Greece. Within days of him arriving in Greece, he unexpectedly passed. So a grieving daughter was another role I assumed.

During this extremely stressful and sad time of my life, I was super duper hard on myself. My thoughts were: I am not being strong enough for my family; I need to give my all to work and help others; I need to work out; I need to lose weight; I need to make sure I am giving all my attention to my son; I can't grieve, I do not have time; I need to navigate the administrative duties following my father's death and not complain; and I need to look presentable and calm every day. I knew I had a lot of blessings and I should have been thankful. But I felt so stressed and detached, I didn't recognize myself. Instead of being kind to myself, I criticized myself and found areas where I could be better—as a wife, mother, leader, daughter, and woman. I hit a point where I was going to crumble. I started listening to podcasts, and all of them mentioned one thing for women—implement self-care and treat ourselves how we would treat our best friends. That means be kind, forgiving, and supportive of ourselves.

I slowly implemented self-care. I woke up a little earlier to work out, even for fifteen minutes. If I could only do five minutes, I did it. I didn't come down hard on myself that I didn't do more than five minutes, but rather congratulated myself on working out. I started to set boundaries for myself and realistic goals to achieve each day. That way, if I did more, I even felt more successful. I learned how to ask for help, and I learned to tell myself I was doing a great job.

I still fail on a daily basis and hear my inner critic. I actively work hard to keep that critic at bay. I appreciate that I push myself, but a close friend pointed out that I am way too hard on myself. So I try to find a balance. It is a battle every day, but I will defeat that critic eventually. My victory will be final, and my inner womenemy will be defeated when I am able to see the phenomenal woman that I am.

<u>Lesson:</u> Be Your Own Best Friend

Uplift yourself and support yourself just like you would your best friend. As all positive change starts from within, when you defeat your inner womenemy, you will be more likely to eliminate instances where you are a womenemy to other women.

Conclusion

The Women's Code/The Gals' Guide

Thank you for reading this book. I hope you took something from it. I want to note that every woman I discuss in this book, even the ones who have done some negative things, are good people who have, like all of us, just made some bad choices. I fully believe the women in this book, and all women, have the power to eliminate the instances where they are womenemies. We all have been a womenemy. I definitely have—numerous times. By writing this book, I have become more aware of the issues presented to us as a gender and notice myself exercising better judgment when put in situations where if I am not careful, I could be a womenemy to another woman.

I have noticed that the women who have been victims of a womenemy turn around and sometimes become the same type of womenemy to another woman. Just because one woman goes through it doesn't mean it has to be a rite of passage. This is not a sorority house where everyone needs to be hazed. This is our lives, our livelihood, our experiences, and our relationships. The more supportive and caring we can be toward another woman, the closer we are to slaying the different types of womenemies in the world.

I wanted to sum up some good rules to follow, and hopefully we can eliminate womenemies and have a new movement: #Wom-enlightenment.

1. **Keep your friends' secrets in the strictest confidence.**

2. **Don't get mad at your friends for keeping others' secrets.**

3. **Don't be the other woman.**

4. **If you find out you are the other woman, end the relationship.**

5. **Counsel your friend not to be the other woman.**

6. **Tell your friend if they are being cheated on.**

7. **Support, uplift and assist women in the workplace.**

8. **Create a warm, loving, and accepting environment for your daughter-in-law.**

9. **Be a supportive, positive, selfless, and trustworthy bridesmaid.**

10. **Avoid hooking up with your friend's ex.**

11. **If you want to date your friend's ex, address it with your friend first.**

12. **Embrace and welcome your significant other's platonic female friends.**

13. **Don't be a womenemy to yourself—be kind, caring, and supportive to yourself. Treat yourself as you would treat your best friend.**

About the Author

Daughter, best friend, wife, mother, Greek, American, Norwegian, vice president, attorney, dancer, cook, and ridiculously enthusiastic Seahawks fan are some of the roles and identities that make up Marilena Fallaris. However when asked who she is, she answers, "A crazy Greek who wants to help others."

Her "on paper" accolades include graduating from the amazing high school that is Lakeside Upper School, graduating from the honors program at the University of Massachusetts

Amherst summa cum laude, graduating Pepperdine Law School magna cum laude, practicing law, being trilingual, being involved in legal marketing, and managing others to be their best in their careers.

Marilena is most proud of the long-lasting connections she has cultivated with family, friends, and colleagues. She tells anyone who will listen how lucky she is to have parents who sent her to Greece every summer to be with her Greek family, friends, and the overall healing way of life that are Greek island summers.

In America as well, she has her amazing, tight-knit community of family, friends, and colleagues. While they are spread throughout the country, the tight-knit feeling comes from the fact that if she ever needs them, they are just a phone call/plane ride/car ride away.

Marilena lives in Los Angeles, on the west side, with her husband and son. She loves being able to help others, whether in the workforce or in personal areas of their lives. In her everyday interactions, she aspires to coach, uplift, and be a resource to others who are trying to be the best version of themselves.

Acknowledgments

Big thanks to GOD for granting me this opportunity at life, love, and the ability to meet so many amazing people. Thank you for being my constant source of faith, even when my world felt as if it was falling apart.

To my mom, Katherine – thank you for always being my cheerleader and for being a rock star of a human being who is always taking care of so many people in your life. Also, thank you for showing me the joy of writing as you are a superb writer. Hopefully the world will see that talent soon!

To my husband, Vasilis – thank you for loving me through the good, the bad, and the unknown. Thank you for believing in me during the moments I was at my lowest level of confidence. Thank you for being my push to get this book out there.

To my son, Emmanuel – thank you for being born and for reminding us how simple things make us the happiest in life. Your joy for life is contagious.

To my dad in heaven – thank you for always showing me the importance of and the joy that comes from helping and inspiring others. Thank you for being full of life when you were here and honoring me with the best father-daughter dance in the universe! Here is the clip: https://vimeo.com/205744133. Note: after the slow song, the dancing goes into hip hop and some Greek dancing!

To Dan – while God gave me one biological father, he gave me another father figure in you. Thank you for your unwavering support and for your ability to stay calm through all my stressful moments.

To Grandma Barbara – thank you for being the kindest person I know. Thank you for teaching me to forgive, to keep my faith in God, and to always be thankful for what I have. You are a special soul and I am blessed to be related to you.

To my cousin Costas – thank you for all the love and care you show through your daily actions. I never felt I had a cousin in you, I felt I had a brother. You have been my rock of strength when I needed it the most.

To my papou Costas – thank you for making the amazing summers in Greece a reality. Thank you for showing me what true love is – the love you shared with yiayia Mary is what I strived to find (and thank God I did). Thank you for showing us that age ain't nothing but a number – dancing it up at 92!

To my yiayia Mary in heaven – thank you for instilling in me the love for cooking, dancing, music, family, and the sea. I am honored to be named after you.

To my immediate family in Greece and the US – Mom, Dad, Dan, Vasilis, Emmanuel, Yiayia Mary in heaven, Papou Costa, Theo Christos, Thea Evi, Costas, Fania, Zeta, Georgos, Marina, Anna, Grandma Barbara, Aunt Sarah, Aunt Carol, Aunt Shio, Uncle Sam, Uncle David, Uncle Toby, Taku, Sophie, and Chloe – thank you for providing unconditional love and countless amazing memories and adventures.

To my extended family (I am Greek and Norwegian, so there are lots!) – thank you for making, or attempting to make, each interaction we have a positive one.

To Angela – thank you for your constant love, for being always there for me, and for being a person I can just sit with in silence. Our families go back generations, and I hope we continue the tradition of best friends through our children, grandchildren, great-grandchildren, etc.

To Akilah- it makes sense we are only two days apart. Your energy, sense of humor, vulnerability and care are contagious. Thank you for being my Seahawks watching sister and for all the texts messages and phone conversations that have fed my soul.

To Jemimah – thank you for your constant positivity, calmness, ability to listen to my overly dramatic stories and for always making me feel safe to express myself. PS- thank you for putting up with the thousands of group text messages from me and Akilah discussing every Seahawks game☐

To Steve – Thank you for allowing me to vent, overexpress and try to figure myself out. Thank you for the endless hours of study sessions in law school, for helping me get out of an unhealthy situation, for the many late nights dancing, and for our made-up song of "doh doh doh".

To Sahar – thank you for being my roomie for almost a decade, for pushing me to put myself first at times, for being protective of me, and for repeatedly telling me the importance of being happy and that life and family are more important than anything.

To Christiana – thank you for introducing me to my husband, for our endless positive dance memories, for your pursuit to heal others with sound baths, and for your positive vibes. Thank you for being there for me during the happiest and saddest parts of my life.

To Doxa – you are the definition of a selfless friend. From driving over an hour to put together our baby furniture, to cooking for me when I was dealing with being an overwhelmed mother, to creating my website, you do everything from love. Thank you for everything that you do.

To Nandia – thank you for the daily texts, for being someone with whom I have shared my motherhood emotions and concerns, and for all the amazing Agiokambos memories we have had and will have.

To Titika – thank you for always showing me there is something to smile about in even the hardest situations. As I said to Nandia, thank you for all the amazing Agiokambos memories we have had and will have.

To Spiros – thank you for checking in on me exactly when I need it, even when I do not ask for it.

To Dean – thank you for your endless positivity and zest for life…and for being my first friend I met at church!

To Cartier – thank you for being there when I needed to talk, for your solid advice, and for making me laugh by sending silly photos of Michael.

To Michael – thank you for over two decades of friendship and for the levity you have brought to my life.

To Valarie, George, Takis, Joanne – thank you for being my surrogate Greek family in California and for the amazing tzatziki!!!

To Ken & Betty – thank you for your love, support and kindness. I have learned so much from you, in business and in life, and am truly grateful to have you in my life.

To Connie and Ashley – thank you for your unwavering friendship and support during one of our darkest hours. Thank you for your mentorship, love and the happy environment you provide every time we see you.

Nick & Marie – thank you for always being so positive but at the same time caring and supportive. Your energy is contagious and we enjoy our trips together.

To my Godmother Zeta and Godsister Marina – thank you for being a listening ear whenever I needed to vent, ask for help, or request advice. Your calmness and ability to love are effortless.

To Karen – thank you for inspiring me and modeling the type of leader I want to be.

To Lisa – thank you for your mentorship, love, kick in the butt, and for being 100 percent YOU all the time.

To Stacee – thank you for always being there. I am so happy our work friendship turned into life friendship.

To Kaveh – thank you for your friendship, your big heart, and allowing me to learn so much from you.

To Rebecca – thank you for being welcoming to all, caring to all, and for truly wanting everyone around you to be happy.

To my friends Angela, Jason, Nandia, Titika, Marina, Akilah, Jemimah, Sahar, Christiana, Doxa, Annie, Connie, Ashley, Nicole, Steve, Spiros, Valarie, George, Dean, Angelo, Katherine, Jeanne, Rosi, Julie, Kevin, Signe, Dan, Helen, Cartier, Michael, Lucas, Denise, Jessica, Ashlee, Natasha, Mark, Karla, Lulu, Charlie, Karen, Lisa, Danny, Danielle, Jackie, Anastasia, Michalis, Tracy, Roylan, Natalie, Claire, Stella, Lydia, Dina, Shannon, Renee, Alex, Cairo, Jonathan, Jo,

Jason, Nick, Marie, Jennifer, Konstantinos, Marta, Tiffany, Vangelis, Tori, Anastasios, Geri, Sarah, Anne, Reggie, Michael, Michele, Frank, Erica, Mara, Aris, Karen, Vered, Liz, Cathy, Sherman, Nina, Jimmy, Teresa, Kaveh, Rebecca, Gina, Dieter, Stacee, Jose, Takis, Joanne, Ken, and Betty – thank you for being my tribe and being a listening ear, a kick in the butt when I needed it, and a source of extreme happiness for me. Though I don't talk to all of you all the time, I always feel your constant support and love.

To Konstantinos Mousoulis – for shining light on the fact that I love to write and for encouraging that love.

To Abdul – thank you for being the most positive person I know. You are wise beyond your years. Thank you for your continuous love and support of our family!

To Annie – I am so happy our friendship started over my love of feta and finding it at your store! Thank you for the countless adventures, for making me giggle, and for your friendship.

To Pinky Lilani & Women of the Future Awards – thank you Pinky for inspiring women to be leaders and for creating the Women of the Future Awards to celebrate the awesomeness of women!

To the awesome people I have worked with and continue to work with – you have been integral in my growth and I appreciate learning from you on the daily. I consider you part of my friendship/family circle!

To Demetra and Nicole – you two read my book in its very first draft and gave me the positive encouragement to share my story with the world.

To Cathy – more than doing my hair, you are my therapist, friend, encourager and source of positive energy. Thanks to you and Courtney at Hush Hush Bang Bang for helping me take, and get ready for, my photo for this book!

To Roxana – nanny doesn't describe your job. Angel/lifeline is better suited. Thank you for watching our baby boy and giving him so much love during one of the most difficult years of our lives. Thank you for teaching us how to be better parents. You are our family.

To Paul Brodie – thank you for making my publishing dreams come true and being an awesome coach!

To Belinda from Working From Your Happy Place – thank you for your awesome podcast, which introduced me to Paul Brodie and made publishing this book possible.

To Maria Menounos & Better Together Podcast – you haven't met me, but your phenomenal podcast touched and inspired me during one of the hardest times of my life. It has been my daily therapy and self-care regimen. Thank you for the reminder that life happens for us and not to us.

To the reader – thank you for taking the time to read this, it means a whole lot to me.

To the women I mentioned in this book – thank you for all the lessons you have taught me over the years. To the friends who are mentioned in the lesson aspect of this book, thank you for role modeling the ideal behavior we should integrate in our daily lives.

Contact Information

Marilena can be reached at marilena@womenemies.com
Website: www.womenemies.com
Follow Marilena on Instagram: @asterimarilena
Follow Marilena on Twitter: @AsteriMarilena
Follow Marilena on Facebook : Marilena Fallaris-Psyrras
Connect with Marilena on LinkedIn: Marilena Fallaris

Request for Feedback

Thank you for taking the time to read my book. I found it cathartic, healing, and eye-opening to write about my own experiences. I believe women have many stories about dealing with womenemies, and I would love to hear your stories so we can tackle eliminating the existence of all womenemies and support our fellow sisters! Please submit any stories to marilena@womenemies.com. Let's affect some change!